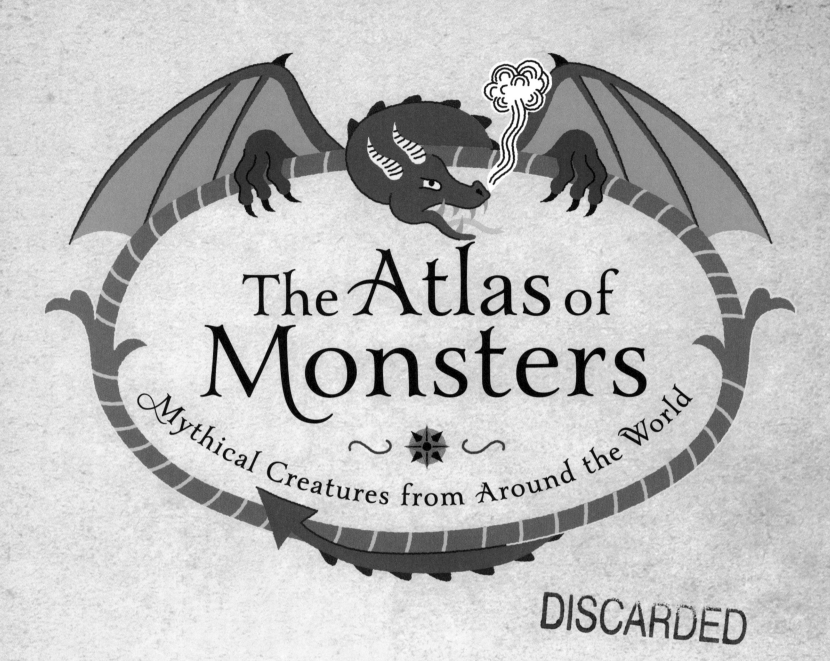

# The Atlas of Monsters

*Mythical Creatures from Around the World*

Written by Sandra Lawrence

Illustrated by Stuart Hill

BPP

Ruth Briggs
Librarian
Hardacre Manor
Berkshire

2nd July

Edmund Wright, Editor
Mercator and Co
Mapmakers
Bloomsbury
London

Dear Mr Wright,

I am writing to you as librarian of Hardacre Manor, Berkshire, about an extraordinary discovery that I have made on the estate.

Hardacre's late owner, Professor Magnus Hardacre, was a great collector of antique manuscripts, especially the poetry of the 16th century recluse, Cornelius Walters (1542 – 1616).

Sadly, Professor Hardacre passed away a year ago. We had seen little of him before he died; he seemed preoccupied with a matter he did not disclose to his staff. After a quiet funeral I began cataloguing the professor's collection of Cornelius Walters' poetry for auction. It was not expected to fetch a large sum; Walters was not considered the best poet of his age — in fact he is often considered a very bad one.

While cataloguing, I tripped and fell against a Tudor beam. To my astonishment, the wall gave way, revealing a secret hiding place.

The cavity was dusty, dirty and filled with cobwebs. As my eyes adjusted to the light, they fell upon an ancient chest, secured with iron bands and a large padlock. Recent fingerprints around the keyhole showed I was not the first person in 400 years to stumble on this place. Professor Hardacre had got there first.

The box contained a bundle of papers from Cornelius Walters' youth. To my great excitement this was not more poetry but an atlas, written and illustrated by Walters himself. In it, Walters describes strange, secret creatures from all over the world — almost as though he had seen them himself.

Authors going all the way back to ancient Greece and Rome filled gaps in their knowledge using travellers' tales and their imaginations. The most famous is probably the ancient Roman historian Pliny the Elder, (AD 23–79) who wrote **Naturalis Historia** (Natural History), which has a section on animals that contains many fantastical beasts. I expected a similar work.

Reading these pages, however, I found myself puzzled. Cornelius Walters writes as though he really had travelled the globe, logging the Earth's mythical creatures. Surely this is impossible; the monsters he describes are the dragons and vampires of myth, folklore and imagination.

Walters clearly intended to share his atlas with the world, so why did he hide it away and spend the rest of his days writing dreadful poetry? I am puzzled. Even though few believe these creatures are real today, the extent of Walters' travels would have made him as famous as Sir Walter Raleigh or Sir Francis Drake, the great explorers of this era.

I enclose here the results of my research. I have reproduced Walters' maps and log, overlaying modern international borders and place names for clarity. Amongst Walters' descriptions of monsters, there are bizarre symbols, as you will see for yourself.

My first thought was that the entire thing was a forgery. Now I am not so sure. There is a mystery within these pages that eludes me. I find myself believing more and more . . . but no, you will think me fanciful. Sometimes our minds play tricks on us.

I am passing my discoveries to you in the hope your experts may be able to make more sense of them than I have managed. Should they prove of interest, perhaps it is time to publish them so the world can read this extraordinary document. I remain

Yours Truly,

Ruth Briggs

# 1st July, 1563, Mermaid Inn, Southampton

This day is cause for great celebration. I, Cornelius Follywolle Montague Walters, of Great Walters Estate, Berkshire, have at 21 years of age come into my inheritance.

My parents desired me to study the law, but I yearn for adventure and have done since I was a boy, when a wandering poet came to our door. The tales he spun by the fireside were wild stories of fabulous creatures and distant lands.

I have commissioned a ship, the Dragon, to take myself and a crew of hearty souls upon a voyage of discovery.

All are hardy sea dogs, save Hal, the young son of my cook, Will Hardacre, who begged to accompany us. I fear he will be a burden, but in my own youth I would have given my eyes to make such travels. His father promises he is a quick-witted lad, I can only hope this is true.

My intention is to create a mighty volume, an 'atlas' of all the beasts of this earth to share with my fellow human beings.

As yet I know not what my travels will bring. They will certainly not be without danger and it is possible I will not return. I cannot be content until I have seen the marvels of the world with my own eyes.

*Cornelius Walters*

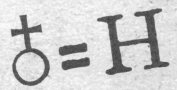

I must add one more thing. This very evening, one night before our departure from Southampton, a messenger knocked at my chamber door with an uncommon note. It is in a script that I have never encountered:

I will mention this to no one; it is bound to be nothing – perhaps a practical joke.

# CONTENTS

Being a list of the contents of this atlas, which depicts the regions of the globe that I, Cornelius Walters, have traversed and where I have catalogued and mapped the monsters found therein.

Is it really possible Walters travelled so far? This is further and wider than anyone had travelled at this time.
— RB

The Orkney Islands

4. *Nuckelavee*

The Shetland Islands

6. *Trow*

*North Atlantic Ocean*

5. *Loch Ness Monster*

*Scotland*

*North Sea*

☿ = R

*Our ship was chased by two such monsters, howling loudly enough to wake the dead.*

1. *Dobhar-Chú*

*Address the Green Man with respect. He is not always as jovial as many think.*

*The Giant's Causeway may be seen here and is a wondrous sight.*

7. *Green Man*

8. *Landlocked Mermaids*

2. *Finn McCool*

*Northern Ireland*

*Irish Sea*

*IRELAND*

12. *Welsh Dragon*

*THE UNITED KINGDOM*

*Here, by a tree, a leprechaun showed me his gold. I marked the tree, yet when I returned, every tree wore the same mark.*

3. *Leprechaun*

9. *Gog and Magog*

*Celtic Sea*

*Wales*

*England*

# Great Britain and Ireland

10. *Cornish Pisky*

11. *Knucker*

*My second mate was led astray by piskies and woke up lost in a bog.*

*English Channel*

12

# Great Britain and Ireland

*The wild and mysterious monsters of these islands have haunted my nightmares since boyhood.*

*If such creatures walk my own homeland, what marvels might be found in the wide world?*

**1. Dobhar-Chú** – This 'water hound' of Ireland travels great distances across land or water, searching for human prey.

**2. Finn McCool** – This Irish warrior giant was born of ancient fairy blood. He is best known for defeating the Scottish giant, Benandonner.

**3. Leprechaun** – Found in Ireland, leprechauns may be dressed in red or green with leather cobblers' aprons, for they are shoemakers. They hide treasure at the end of rainbows. Some will grant wishes, but beware! They love to trick humans.

**4. Nuckelavee** – This creature of the Orkney Islands resembles a horse joined with its rider. The Nuckelavee has neither skin nor hair; instead it is all raw, oozing flesh.

**5. Loch Ness Monster** – This notorious beast lives in the waters of Loch Ness, Scotland, and was first sighted by St Columba in AD 565. It has a large body and long, snake-like neck.

**6. Trow** – Trows come from the northernmost islands of Britain. They are like Nordic trolls, but smaller and they lure human fiddlers to play music in their underground dwellings. Trows cannot live in the sun, so come out only at night.

**7. Green Man** – A spirit of the woodlands, the Green Man is wreathed with leaves and branches. Throughout Britain he is known by many names, including Green George, the Holly Man and Jack-in-the-Green.

**8. Landlocked Mermaids** – Mermaids dwell within the pools of the Peak District. On the high Kinder Scout plateau is a mermaid that will grant immortality. Another, in Black Mere Pool, drags mortals to their deaths.

**9. Gog and Magog** – Gog and Magog are two great giants who guard the City of London. Some say they were captured by the warrior, Brutus, and brought in chains to serve the city.

**10. Cornish Pisky** – Tricky creatures, piskies have red hair and pointed ears. They steal horses and ride them in circles, making fairy rings called 'gallitraps'. Placing both feet in a gallitrap will make you the piskies' prisoner.

**11. Knucker** – This water dragon lives in pools called 'knucker holes'. The knucker hole at Lyminster, West Sussex, was home to a fearsome dragon, which was defeated by a local fellow called Jim Pulk. Jim killed the dragon with a Sussex pudding laced with poison.

**12. Welsh Dragon** – The red dragon is the symbol of Wales. When the fifth-century British king, Vortigern, attempted to build a castle, the building collapsed every night. A young boy called Merlin explained that beneath the tower fought two dragons, red and white. The red dragon eventually defeated the white.

*I cannot remain here. My great desire now is to study the creatures of every part of this earth and record them. I purchased a consignment of vellum for this purpose, but it was consumed by a strange fire. The ashes arranged themselves in a curious fashion:*

*Our ship, the Dragon, left Southampton on the second day of July, 1563. I am certain new wonders await.*

## The Tale of the Giant's Causeway

*The giant Finn McCool made a great pathway, or 'causeway', to Scotland, throwing rocks across the sea. He retreated when he realised how big the Scottish giant Benandonner was. Benandonner crossed to look for Finn, but Finn's wife dressed him as an infant. Benandonner ran away, for if this monstrous baby was the child, how big was the father?*

*The Giant's Causeway may be seen in County Antrim, Northern Ireland.*

1. Trolls of Grímsey

Where there are strange rock formations, there are often stories of trolls and other beings turned to stone. Throughout history, people have needed to explain natural phenomena. — RB

ICELAND

One of this creature's tentacles damaged our main mast.

13. Kraken

Our company sailed many miles out of our way to avoid this peril.

3. Selkie

Norwegian Sea

2. Múshveli

THE FAROE ISLANDS

North Atlantic Ocean

NORWAY

4. Kelpie

We heard kelpies howl before a storm, and their tails clapped like thunder as they hit the water.

12. Lindworm

8. Draugen

North Sea

7. Banshee

Scotland

9. Druon Antigoon

10. Goblin

Northern Ireland

THE UNITED KINGDOM

DENMARK

IRELAND

England

6. Llamhigyn y Dŵr

Wales

5. Black Shuck

NETHERLANDS

11. Brocken Mountain Witches

BELGIUM

GERMANY

POLAND

English Channel

✳ = G

FRANCE

LUXEMBOURG

CZECH REPUBLIC

SWEDEN

15. Andvari

14. Fenrir

Baltic Sea

16. Iku-Turso

FINLAND

17. Antero Vipunen

22. Leshy

White Sea

23. Vodyanoi

We crossed the river safely. Young Hal offered the vodyanoi a present of fish in exchange for safe passage.

ESTONIA

18. Toell the Great

RUSSIA

19. Neringa

$\Psi = A$

LATVIA

LITHUANIA

20. Obra River Monster

21. Wawel Dragon

BELARUS

UKRAINE

Northern Europe

# Northern Europe

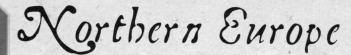

*From my homeland, I sailed around the northern kingdoms of Europe. The creatures of these chilly lands are mysterious and dangerous. Encounters with such beasts are to be avoided, yet my crew was of good cheer.*

**1. Trolls of Grimsey** - These three hideous trolls tried to dig a channel between the Westfjords and the rest of Iceland, but failed to notice the coming dawn. The rising sun turned them to stone; they remain petrified to this day.

**2. Múshveli** - An evil monster of Icelandic waters, the Múshveli, or 'mouse-whale', has razor-sharp teeth and a long tail, like a whip. The beast travels at immense speed.

**3. Selkie** - Selkies are creatures of the Faroe Islands, Scotland, Ireland and Iceland. At sea they take seal form, while on land they resemble humans. From time to time human men take Selkie wives, hiding their seal skins so they may not go back to the sea. This always ends in tragedy.

**4. Kelpie** - Scottish water monsters that appear as horses with flashing eyes, Kelpies haunt fords and lochs. They devour their victims, leaving only entrails floating on the water.

**5. Black Shuck** - This demonic black dog comes from the east of England. On dark nights travellers sense its shaggy coat and icy breath around river banks, marshes and graveyards.

**6. Llamhigyn y Dŵr** - A Welsh water leaper, this beast has a scaly tail and bat wings. It lurks in lakes, dragging fishermen to a watery death.

**7. Banshee** - A fearsome spirit, the banshee is dreaded in Ireland for her haunting screams. She has wild hair and eyes raw from weeping. Seek not to hear the Banshee's wail; she foretells death.

**8. Draugen** - According to Nordic folklore, a draugen is the monstrous ghost of a sailor lost at sea. It is draped entirely with seaweed. Unearthly screams can be heard on stormy nights, as he sinks fishermen's boats.

**9. Druon Antigoon** - In ancient times the giant Druon Antigoon terrorised ship masters of Belgium by demanding a toll to pass through the river Scheldt and cutting off the hands of any who couldn't pay. A Roman warrior named Silvius Brabo killed the giant.

**10. Goblin** - The goblin is found in many countries. In the Netherlands these creatures cause horrifying 'cheese dreams' by sitting on the chests of folk that have eaten cheese before going to bed. The villagers of Drenthe once fought a band of goblins until the sun came up and turned the creatures to stone.

**11. Brocken Mountain Witches** - Once a year, on Walpurgisnacht (May Day eve), witches gather on the Brocken, in Germany's Harz mountains. Arriving by broomstick and goat, they dance through the night.

**12. Lindworm** - This great serpent haunts burial grounds and lonely places. It can shed its skin like a snake and swallow a man whole. Stories of lindworms are found throughout Scandinavia.

**13. Kraken** - An octopus-like monster of the deep sea, the kraken is a creature of Nordic folklore. It causes an almighty whirlwind, dragging ships into its waiting tentacles and swallowing them.

**8.**

**14. *Femir*** - This huge wolf is so dangerous that the Norse gods bound him to a rock. His chains are fairy-made, from the breath of a fish, the footsteps of a cat, the nerves of a bear, the spirit of a bird, the beard of a woman and the roots of a mountain.

**15. *Andvari*** - A dwarf who lives beneath a waterfall, Andvari once possessed a magical ring that brought great wealth. When the Norse god Loki stole the ring, Andvari cursed both it and the gold it summoned.

**16. *Iku-Turso*** - A demonic sea monster, found near Finland, Iku-Turso is the father of all diseases.

**17. *Antero Vipunen*** - An enormous sleeping giant of Finland, Antero Vipunen has slumbered so long that forests grow from the soil he uses as a blanket. As he sleeps, he absorbs wisdom.

**18. *Toell the Great*** - Toell was a giant hero of the island of Saaremaa, Estonia. He fell fighting an evil demon of the underworld called the Great Vile One. His body and head now lie as twisted boulders upon the ground.

**19. *Neringa*** - Neringa was a Lithuanian giantess who built a ribbon of sand dunes to protect some fishermen's homes from a hideous sea dragon. The grateful fisher folk named their town after her.

**20. *Obra River Monster*** - This monstrous creature lurks in the waters of the river Obra in Poland. Some say it resembles a serpent, others a gigantic catfish.

**21. *Wawel Dragon*** - In a cave under Wawel Castle in the ancient city of Kraków, Poland, lived a ferocious man-eating dragon. The beast was defeated by a humble cobbler who fed it sheep coated in sulphur. Its mouth burning, the monster drank so much cooling water from the river Vistula that its stomach exploded.

**22. *Leshy*** - A tricksy spirit of the woods, Leshy often appears as a shaggy old man in green. He leads travellers astray, yet protects wildlife. His laughter can be heard at night. Stories of Leshy are found throughout the Slavic folklore of Eastern Europe.

**23. *Vodyanoi*** - An ancient water spirit of Slavic myth, Vodyanoi appears as a hairy old man on a moss-covered log. The creature lures humans to rivers and ponds then drags them to a watery death.

*After three months in the treacherous northern regions, I ordered my crew to turn south, for winter was approaching. As we prepared to leave, sharp-eyed Hal bid me climb to the crow's nest and look down where, writ upon the ice in deep cracks, was this strange pattern. I know not its purpose. It appears to be some ancient script:*

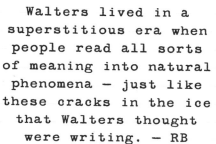

**12.**

**15.**

**20.**

**19.**

**16.**

**21.**

**4.**

**13.**

**9.**

**7.**

**3.**

**17.**

Our ship narrowly missed Hok Braz's grasping arm.

5. Hok Braz

9. Dame Blanche

8. Cheval Mallet

I danced for many hours with this creature.

FRANCE

Southern Europe

Bay of Biscay

7. Tarasque

1. Cuegle

6. Lou Carcolh

ANDORRA

PORTUGAL

From this Moura we won a bag of gold!

SPAIN

3. Comte Arnau

2. El Zangarrón

4. Moura Encantada

We saw the flaming Comte Arnau one thunderous night.

GERMANY

17. Aufhocker

19. Golem

CZECH REPUBLIC

SLOVAKIA

10. Butatsch-cun-Ilgs

LIECHTENSTEIN

11. Krampus

AUSTRIA

18. Tatzelwurm

*A traveller sold me the skeleton of this beast.*

HUNGARY

20. Garabonciá and Zomok

SWITZERLAND

12. Tarantasio

SLOVENIA

CROATIA

BOSNIA & HERZEGOVINA

SERBIA

21. Bukavac

*We blocked our ears from the bukavac's terrible cry.*

*The rib of the Tarantasio is kept in the church of San Bassiano in Pizzighettone.*

MONACO

SAN MARINO

Adriatic Sea

MONTENEGRO

KOSOVO

13. Mouth of Truth

Corsica (France)

VATICAN CITY

ITALY

⊕ = W

Tyrrhenian Sea

15. Pettenedda

Sardinia (Italy)

14. Scylla

ALBANIA

*Lost three good men to these monsters. Catesby, Joiner and Talbot.*

Sicily (Italy)

Strait of Messina

14. Charybdis

Ionian Sea

Mediterranean Sea

16. Acadine

MALTA

19

# Southern Europe

In the treacherous waters and lands of Southern Europe, terrifying creatures may be found. It was not two days before we discovered a new monster for this volume.

**1. Cuegle** – A Cuegle, from Cantabria, Spain, has three glowing eyes and arms with no hands or fingers. Mothers put holly sprigs in their children's cradles to protect them from the beast, which hates this plant.

**2. El Zangarrón** - An enormous giant of the Zamora region, Spain. The people in the village of Sanzoles del Vino dress up as El Zangarrón every year for a parade.

**3. Comte Arnau** - The evil Comte Arnau committed terrible crimes against the poor folk of his lands. He was cursed to gallop for eternity upon an undead horse, followed by demonic dogs. He rides on thunderous nights, wreathed in fire.

**4. Moura Encantada** - These creatures, found near Portugal, have the heads and bodies of beautiful women and the tails of serpents. They have been cursed to guard hoards of treasure and seek humans to release them from their curse.

**5. Hok Braz** – This enormous giant of Brittany, France, has a huge appetite. His name comes from his large, hooked arm. Even after devouring a three-masted galleon, Hok Braz is still hungry.

**6. Lou Carcolh** - This beast has the shell of a snail and lives in the caverns of south-west France. Its slimy tentacles snatch its human prey.

**7. Tarasque** - Found in Provence, southern France, the Tarasque is a dragon-like creature, part-animal, part-fish.

**8. Le Cheval Mallet** - A beautiful demonic horse, found in France, Le Cheval Mallet waits on moonless nights for humans to try to ride it. As soon as the rider mounts, the beast begins to gallop faster than a hurricane. At the end of the night the rider dies of exhaustion or is trampled to death.

**9. Dame Blanche** - These spirits wear white and waylay travellers, asking them to dance. With those who agree they dance solemnly and then vanish. Those that refuse are tormented by the spirits' familiars, which are all manner of night creatures: owls, cats and lutins (hobgoblins). Dames Blanches are found in French folklore.

**10. Butatsch-cun-Ilgs** - Within the Lüschersee, a Swiss Alpine lake, lives the Butatsch-cun-Ilgs. This beast is an enormous blob of flesh in the shape of a cow's stomach, covered in hundreds of blinking eyes.

**11. Krampus** - Half-goat, half-demon, this monster appears during the Christmas season in many countries in this region. He has a sack to carry off naughty children.

**12. Tarantasio** - The Tarantasio was a dragon that terrorised inhabitants around Lake Gerundo, Italy. The lake was drained so the dragon could be killed.

**13. Mouth of Truth** – This is the hideous, marble face of an ancient god, whose gaping mouth will devour the hands of those who have recently lied. It can be seen in the city of Rome.

**14. Scylla and Charybdis** - These two terrible monsters live on either side of the narrow Strait of Messina, between Italy and Sicily. Sailors must choose which of them to risk.

**15. Pettenedda** - This old hag lives at the bottom of wells in Sardinia. Her hair is so matted she spends eternity combing it. Children that fall into her well are forced to comb her hair forever.

**16. Acadine** - A magical fountain in Sicily, the Acadine will tell truth from lies. Throw any piece of writing into the waters; if it tells the truth, the paper will float. If not it will sink.

**17. Aufhocker** - Found in the forests of Germany, the Aufhocker's name means 'leap upon' and comes from the way it attacks. It jumps upon its victims' backs and tears out their throats. It can take the shape of a black dog, a horse or even a human.

**18.** *Tatzelwurm* - The Tatzelwurm is two metres long with a scaly, snake-like body and a cat-like head. It breathes fumes of poison and lives in mountain crevices.

**19.** *Golem* - A golem is a creature made from mud and brought to life by magic to serve its master. When its name is removed, it crumbles back into dust. It is found in Jewish folklore and the most famous golem was made in Prague in the Czech Republic.

10.

**20.** *Garaboncia and Zomok* - Garabonciás are great magicians of Hungary. They have learned to capture and ride Zomok: dragons that create thunderstorms with their wings.

**21.** *Bukavac* - This horned, six-legged monster lives in water, either in lakes or ponds. It makes a terrifying noise before it strangles its prey. 'Buka' means 'noise' in Croatian.

## Tales of the Beasts of Southern Europe

*These stories were told to me by the many wise people of these lands. I attach my notes for safekeeping.*

18.

19.

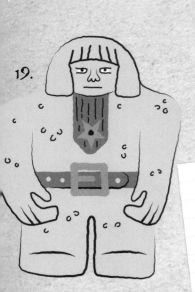

*We travelled boldly through these lands for more than three months and now journey on, towards the islands of Greece.*

*As we sailed away from the terrible Scylla, a great pile of seaweed appeared upon the top deck of my ship. Young Hal was about to remove it when I noticed it formed mysterious shapes, copied here:*

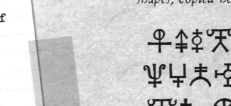

*As yet I know not what they might mean.*

> A photograph of a forged Tatzelwurm skeleton turned up at the Geneva Institute of Science in the early 1900s. Could this be the one Walters mentions on the map? The bones themselves are now missing. — RB

### Martha and the Tarasque

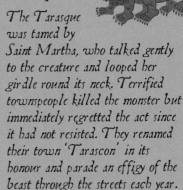

*The Tarasque was tamed by Saint Martha, who talked gently to the creature and looped her girdle round its neck. Terrified townspeople killed the monster but immediately regretted the act since it had not resisted. They renamed their town 'Tarascon' in its honour and parade an effigy of the beast through the streets each year.*

### The Golem of Prague

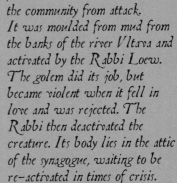

*I have seen the body of the famous golem created in Prague to protect the community from attack. It was moulded from mud from the banks of the river Vltava and activated by the Rabbi Loew. The golem did its job, but became violent when it fell in love and was rejected. The Rabbi then deactivated the creature. Its body lies in the attic of the synagogue, waiting to be re-activated in times of crisis.*

14.

7.

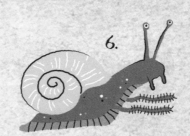

6.

20.

12.

> Walters seems convinced the seaweed formed a message! He would have learned of the legendary Greek hero Odysseus in school, and appears to attribute the loss of his three men to Scylla and Charybdis, creatures Odysseus faced. However, he doesn't say that he actually saw either hazard. — RB

### Scylla and Charybdis

*Scylla, once a beautiful water nymph, was turned to a hideous sea monster by a jealous sorceress. She is a writhing mass of tentacles with many heads. Charybdis is ever-thirsty and swallows vast amounts of water before spitting it out in a perilous whirlpool.*

4.

21.

**3. Werewolf**

There is only one way to kill a werewolf: a silver bullet.

HUNGARY

**1. Vampire**

Vampires cannot stand the smell of garlic.

MOLDOVA

CROATIA

**4. Svyatogor**

I met Svyatogor here, though he is known throughout Slavic stories.

ROMANIA

**2. Balaur**

BOSNIA AND HERZEGOVINIA

SERBIA

KOSOVO

Black Sea

Herakles is not a monster, but a hero who has defeated many beasts.

BULGARIA

**10. Herakles**

MACEDONIA

ALBANIA

**5. Centaur**

Sea of Marmara

**6. Harpy**

Ionian Sea

Aegean Sea

TURKEY

GREECE

**9. Chimera**

**7. Cyclops**

**8. Minotaur**

Crete (Greece)

Mediterranean Sea

# South-East Europe

Ƶ = D

# South-East Europe

The terrifying oceans of these realms are nothing to the perils lurking on land. The beasts to be encountered in Greece are especially to be feared.

*1. Vampire* - One that has died, yet is not dead. The 'undead' roam at night, drinking human blood from their victims' necks. They are found throughout this region.

*2. Balaur* - An evil, many-headed snake-creature that eats humans. It is found in Romania.

*3. Werewolf* - A werewolf is a man that transforms into a monster on nights when the moon is full. Wielding superhuman strength, the wolf-beast is satisfied only by human flesh. Werewolves are common throughout Europe.

*4. Svyatogor* - A giant of immense strength, Svyatogor met a tragic end. He discovered a magic bag so heavy he could not lift it. After straining many hours, he forced his body into the ground, where he died.

*5. Centaur* - Half-man, half-horse, these fierce creatures roam the mountains and forests of Greece. Centaurs can be wise and generous, but have quick tempers.

*6. Harpy* - Horrific storm spirits, harpies have the bodies of vultures and the faces of wild women. Their wings and talons are made of brass.

*7. Cyclops* - Cyclopses are hideous, one-eyed giants of Greece. The most notorious, Polyphemus, captured the hero Odysseus and his crew. While the giant slept, Odysseus' men blinded him so they could escape.

*8. Minotaur* - King Minos of Crete built an unsolvable labyrinth to contain the Minotaur, a half-man, half-bull that ate human flesh. Prince Theseus of Athens killed the monster with help from Minos's daughter Ariadne, who gave the hero a ball of wool to find his way out of the maze.

*9. Chimera* - This fire-breathing monster left a trail of destruction through Turkey. It has the head of a lion, the tail of a serpent and the body of a goat. It was slain by the hero Bellerophon, riding the winged horse, Pegasus.

*One might study the creatures of this land for a lifetime, yet the lands beyond beckoned and we set our course further east. As we hoisted the sails, a host of strange birds flocked, tearing at the canvas with their beaks. The slashes they made haunt my dreams:*

✶✝☥⚶  ☖⚄⚇⊙
⚅⚶✳⊙⚉⊙⚐⚶
⚇⚉⊙
⚷✝☖⚅⚉⊶✝⚇⊙⚉⊹

## The trials of HERAKLES

*10. Herakles* – The Greek hero, Herakles, was ordered to fulfil twelve tasks as penance for the murder of his family in a fit of madness. His tasks included the defeat of some terrifying monsters – too many to map on this atlas. Here I list the most fearsome.

*The Nemean Lion*

A gigantic lion that could not be killed with iron, bronze or stone. Herakles strangled it with his bare hands.

*The Lernaean Hydra*

A many-headed sea monster. Whenever Herakles cut off one head, two more would grow. Finally he burned each wound so the heads could not regrow. The last head was immortal so he buried it under a rock.

*Geryon*

Herakles had to capture the cattle belonging to Geryon, a three-headed herdsman with three sets of legs and a terrifying dog.

*The Stymphalian birds*

These vicious birds have beaks and claws of bronze, and toxic dung. Protected by the skin of the Nemean Lion, Herakles killed the creatures.

*Cerberus*

The three-headed guard dog of the underworld. Herakles captured the beast, but later allowed it to return to its post.

Barents Sea

Kara Sea

ħ = P.

1. Kreutzet

7. Upir

2. Baba Faga

We stood in awe
at the foot of these
great rocks.

6. Manpupuner Giants

8. Firebird

3. Kikimora
and Domovoi

To appease an angry kikimora,
Hal washed all our pots and
pans with fern tea.

5. Palesmurt

4. Solovei Rakhmatich

Curse Solovei Rakhmatich.
He has stolen my purse!

9. Zmey

16. Griffin

KAZAKHSTAN

MONGOLIA

UKRAINE

15. Azrail

Black Sea

GEORGIA

Caspian Sea

UZBEKISTAN

KYRGYZSTAN

CHINA

TURKEY

ARMENIA

AZERBAIJAN

TURKMENISTAN

IRAN

AFGHANISTAN

TAJIKISTAN

17. Feti Ögüz
(Seven Bulls)

Laptev Sea

East Siberian Sea

Ϧ = 0

14. Shurale

11. Kozei

11. Kutkh

RUSSIA

10. Alklba

13. Almas

12. Kamali
We saw great blasts of fire
erupt from the mountains as the
Kamali wreaked havoc.

Sea of
Okhotsk

Sea of Japan

NORTH
KOREA

SOUTH
KOREA

JAPAN

# Russia and Central Asia

It's extraordinary that Walters made it so far.
Even today some of these regions are difficult to reach.
Did he really visit? Could he just be a good liar? — RB

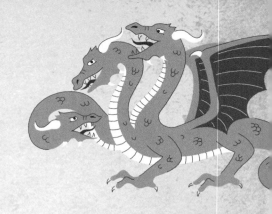

# Russia and Central Asia

Onwards, to the northern regions of the East. Some parts here are very remote and the people tell stories of wild things hiding in the snow-capped mountains and dark forests. Creatures of earth, air and fire, these beasts are highly dangerous.

**1. Kreutzet** - This enormous bird of north-west Russia resembles an eagle, though it is of a much greater size.

**2. Baba Jaga** - A fearsome witch of Slavic Folklore ('Slavic' describes a group of people from Eastern Europe linked by their customs and language), Baba Jaga has iron teeth, is skinny as a skeleton and is always ravenous for human blood. She lives in a hut that walks on chicken legs and has a fence of her victims' skulls.

**3. Kikimora and Domovoi** - Household spirits found in Russia, domovoi are small and bearded. They are often married to kikimora, spirits who look after chickens and keep the house. They are usually protective but can get ill tempered and start throwing things in a badly kept home.

3.

**4. Solovei Rakhmatich** - This half-man, half-bird used to perch in a gigantic tree over the pass between Chernigov and Kiev, in the Ukraine. It would screech at passers-by, killing them and stealing their belongings.

**5. Palesmurt** - This bizarre monster is found near the river Volga. It has half a body, one arm, one hand, one leg, one foot and a head with one eye. The palesemurt ensnares travellers and strangles them to death.

**6. Manpupuner Giants** - These seven rock giants are found in north-west Russia, frozen atop a snowy peak. They were marching across the mountain to conquer the neighbouring Mansi people. On seeing the holy Mansi Mountains, the leader dropped his drum and all seven were turned to stone.

**7. Upir** - Some call these creatures werewolves, others believe they are vampires, but all agree they are dangerous. They sleep during the day in Russia's graveyards and hunt human prey at night.

7.

**8. Firebird** - This bird from Slavic legend is not unlike a peacock, but its plumage glows with the colours of fire. Just one feather will light up a large room with red, orange and yellow.

**9. Zmey** - There are a great many dragons in these lands, where they are called zmey. One of the fiercest of all was Tugarin Zmey. The hero Alyosha Popovich fought the monster, but was unable to beat it until a thunderstorm ripped its wings and the creature crashed to earth where Popovich cut off its head.

**10. Alklha** - A dragon spoken of by the Buryat people of Siberia, Alklha is so vast that its wings cover the sky. It nibbles at the moon, taking a bite each day but cannot contain it and vomits it back up. Alklha occasionally tries to eat the sun, but it is too hot.

**11. Kutkh and Kozei** - The great peninsula of Kamchatka was made when Kutkh, the raven spirit, dropped a feather while riding in his dog-sled. The mountains were forged when Kozei, the dog, shook snow from his coat, causing an earthquake.

**12. Kamali** - These demons live in volcanoes in the Kamchatka Peninsula in east Russia. If humans venture too close to their hunting grounds they explode, creating havoc and death.

**13. Almas** - These giants are very shy of humans and are covered in shaggy fur. Rarely sighted, their booming call haunts Siberia.

**14. Shurale** - A mischievous monster of the forests, Shurale has a furry body and a single horn in his head. He hides in the trees, waiting for victims to pass, then tickles them to death. He appears in the folklore of Russia's Tatar and Bashkir peoples.

**15. Azrail** - This terrible giant of Armenia was outwitted by a wandering apprentice. The young man chopped off Azrail's head, which he then cut in half. The head goaded him to strike a third time but the apprentice refused, as a third stroke would have restored Azrail to life.

**16. Griffin** - A great bird with the head and legs of an eagle and the body of a lion, the griffin is big enough to block out the sun. Griffins guard hoards of treasure and line their nests with gold. They are found in many countries; we heard tales of them in the gold mines of this region.

**17. Jeti Ögüz (Seven Bulls)** - These seven giant bulls of Kyrgyztan were turned to stone when a jealous king killed his wife. Her blood drowned her murderer and turned the bulls into the blood-red rocks of the canyon.

*The beasts of these regions were wary of humans and are dangerous when disturbed. Wherever we journeyed, we found ominous cracks in the frost; always with the same eerie configuration.*

Sometimes Tugarin is remembered not as a Zmey but as an evil giant. — RB

Walters records these markings with great care. Could he really be telling the truth after all? Maybe he did indeed see strange marks, but did they mean anything? — RB

1. Manzaširi

3. Bixi

KAZAKHSTAN

KYRGYZSTAN

UZBEKISTAN

TAJIKISTAN

AFGHANISTAN

4. Shangyang

5. Jiangshi

6. Sun Wukong

C H I N A

7. Xiangliu

PAKISTAN

TIBET

Here we attended a
mighty feast for the
ogre Gurumapa.

NEPAL

BHUTAN

18. Yeti

17. Gurumapa

BANGLADESH

China and
Central
Asia

I N D I A

MYANMAR
(BURMA)

Walters may have read about this region in the writings of Marco Polo, a Venetian merchant-adventurer who journeyed to China in the 13th century. — RB

MONGOLIA

2. *Mongolian Death Worm*

8. *Xiezhi*

9. *Xingtian*

10. *Nian*

LAOS

*Gulf of Tonkin*

12. *Yinglong*

14. *Qilin*

Some say the *Qilin* has a single horn; others believe it grows antlers.

11. *Huli Jing*

Yellow Sea

NORTH KOREA

SOUTH KOREA

Sea of Japan

16. *Dokkaebi*

✠ = L

East China Sea

13. *Longwang*

15. *Hai Ho Shang*

TAIWAN

*Hal and I performed the ritual dance and saved our crew from the Hai Ho Shang.*

The lands of this region are vast, mysterious and dangerous. Within the high mountains, desert plains and dense forests we encountered monsters so hideous I shiver as I write.

**1. Manzaśiri** - This giant of Mongolia is so huge that his body became the earth. His eyes became the sun and moon and his blood turned to rivers. Volcanoes and earthquakes rise from the heat of his internal organs.

1.

2.

**2. Mongolian Death Worm** - This giant worm lives in the Gobi Desert of Mongolia and attacks humans and animals. Its slimy coils squirt deadly venom. The beast travels underground by burrowing through the sand.

**3. Bixi** - Bixi has the shell of a tortoise and a love of literature. To touch a statue of Bixi brings good luck and Bixi statues are often seen in temples in China.

**4. Shangyang** - This enormous bird of China has one leg and is known as the 'rain bird'. Some say it dances upon its single leg to conjure storms, others claim it sucks water from rivers with its beak, then sprays it over the fields.

**5. Jiangshi** - These hopping vampire-zombies kill humans to absorb their life-force. They move only by night, hiding from the daylight in coffins and caves throughout China.

**6. Sun Wukong** - Sun Wukong, the Monkey King, is a mischievous trickster of Chinese folklore. He is a skilled fighter and once made a famous journey to the west with a monk, a fish spirit and a greedy pig spirit to find wisdom.

**7. Xiangliu** - This horrific snake had nine heads. Its excrement was so vile it turned lakes and rivers into stinking swamps and, when it was finally slain by the hero Yu the Great, its blood poisoned the land.

**8. Xiezhi** - Though this single-horned monster is of horrifying appearance, it has a great love for justice. It will distinguish between human truth and falsehood. It punishes the wicked and can reveal the guilty party in a dispute.

**9. Xingtian** - This giant has no head but his eyes and mouth are on his chest. He is the mortal enemy of the Yellow Emperor of Chinese legend.

**10. Nian** - A terrible demon-monster that lives in the mountains, Nian appears at Chinese New Year.

**11. Huli Jing** - Fox spirits of China take many forms. They are wise and scholarly, but may also be tricksters and shape-changers. After 1000 years they turn white or silver and sprout nine tails.

**12. Yinglong** - This unusual variety of long has fur instead of scales, and feathered wings. It is said a Yinglong stopped the Yellow River of China flooding by forming channels with its tail.

**13. Longwang** - Longwang are the four dragon kings that reign over the North, South, East and West Seas. People make gifts to them when rain is needed.

15.

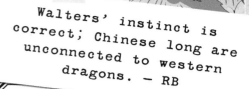

Walters' instinct is correct; Chinese long are unconnected to western dragons. - RB

### Chinese Long

Although they look similar, with legs, scales and claws, I can only conclude Chinese long, such as Yinglong and Longwang are mere distant cousins to the fire-breathing dragons of Europe. Wise and powerful, these majestic animals are deeply respected in China. There are nine kinds of long, controlling different aspects of the universe.

10.

13.

14.

9.

7.

5.

17.

16.

**14. Qilin** - This beast has flaming scales and the body of a horse. Despite its terrifying appearance, the Qilin is a gentle creature. It walks on clouds rather than harm the grass and eats only leaves. It foretells the birth of great heroes and wise rulers of China. Sighting one brings good luck.

**15. Hai Ho Shang** - This sea monster drags entire junks (a type of Chinese ship) underwater, drowning all on board. Sailors burn feathers if one is sighted, for it cannot stand the smell. To be sure of warding it off, however, an intricate dance must be performed to the ritual beat of a gong.

**16. Dokkaebi** - These tricksy goblins, found in Korea, can make themselves invisible to play pranks. They often challenge travellers to wrestling matches, and will steal from the greedy, giving the wealth to people who deserve it.

**17. Gurumapa** - A terrifying ogre, the Gurumapa has monstrous fangs. It is found in Nepal.

**18. Yeti** - A shaggy, ape-like beast, the yeti lives in the mountains, walking upright like a human. It climbs to high areas in the Himalayas searching for a particular, salty moss that grows on the rocks.

*The strange signs from the monsters whirl around my head at night, denying me sleep. Why will they not leave me alone? As we left the Yellow River, a sudden waterspout smashed two junks, leaving them nothing but driftwood floating in those infernal patterns:*

*I believe the beasts are angry.*

I have studied many ancient languages and this resembles nothing I have seen. What am I saying? Of course it doesn't. Monsters do not leave messages because they don't exist! — RB

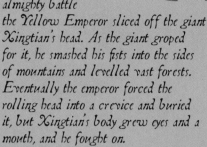

## Tales of the Beasts of China and Central Asia

### Xingtian and the Yellow Emperor

*During an almighty battle the Yellow Emperor sliced off the giant Xingtian's head. As the giant groped for it, he smashed his fists into the sides of mountains and levelled vast forests. Eventually the emperor forced the rolling head into a crevice and buried it, but Xingtian's body grew eyes and a mouth, and he fought on.*

### The Tale of Nian

*Every year, on the first day of the first month, Nian would descend on the village, devouring the crops and kidnapping children. One day a god, disguised as an old man, told the villagers Nian's secret fears – loud noises and the colour red. Each Chinese New Year, people deck their houses in red, crash pots and pans and light firecrackers to ward him off.*

### The Tale of the Gurumapa

*A lazy gambler called Kesha Chandra persuaded Gurumapa to carry a pot of gold for him. In return he said the ogre could devour all the village's naughty children. Gurumapa took the children and the villagers were furious. They saved them by making an agreement with the ogre. Once a year they hold a great feast in his honour so he is too full to eat humans.*

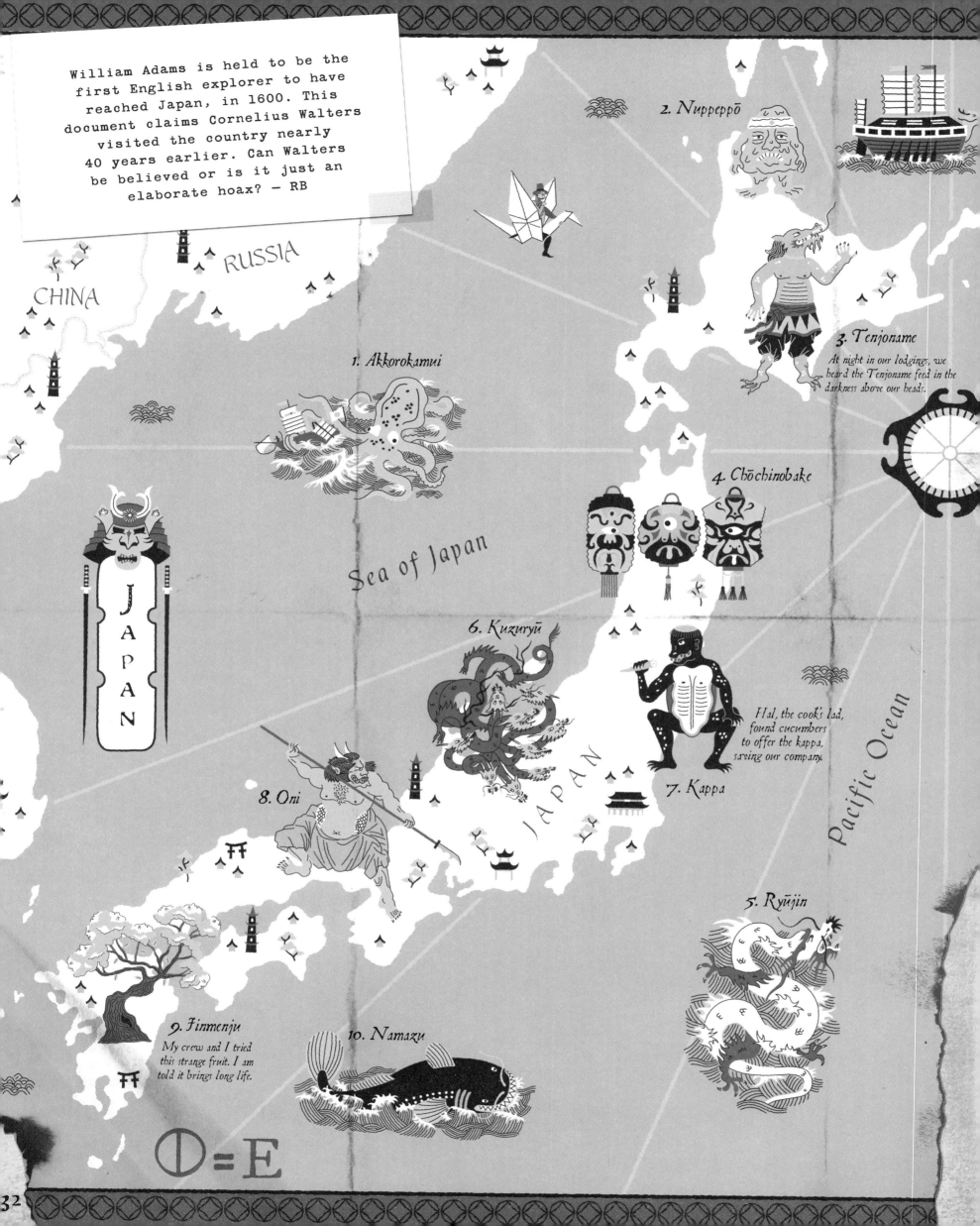

William Adams is held to be the first English explorer to have reached Japan, in 1600. This document claims Cornelius Walters visited the country nearly 40 years earlier. Can Walters be believed or is it just an elaborate hoax? — RB

CHINA

RUSSIA

2. Nuppeppō

3. Tenjoname

*At night in our lodgings, we heard the Tenjoname feed in the darkness above our heads.*

1. Akkorokamui

Sea of Japan

4. Chōchinobake

JAPAN

6. Kuzuryū

*Hal, the cook's lad, found cucumbers to offer the kappa, saving our company.*

7. Kappa

Pacific Ocean

8. Oni

JAPAN

5. Ryūjin

9. Jinmenju

*My crew and I tried this strange fruit. I am told it brings long life.*

10. Namazu

$\Phi = E$

# Japan

The creatures of these lands are many and terrifying. To add to the large number of demons and other monsters, when a household object reaches its one hundredth year of existence it is rewarded with life. Yōkai, or mysterious spirits, are to be encountered in every nook and cranny.

*1. Akkorokamui* – A sea monster like an enormous octopus, the Akkorokamui is red and emits a terrible stench. Akkorokamui drag fishermen and their boats underwater. If one of its coiling tentacles is severed, the limb will regrow. The Ainu people of northern Japan tell of Akkorokamui in their legends.

*2. Nuppeppō* – This globulous, fatty blob hangs around streets and quiet places. Nuppeppō are not dangerous, though they often smell of rotting flesh.

*3. Tenjoname* – The 'ceiling-licker' is a tall, skinny monster with a very long, filthy tongue. It lurks in the corners of houses waiting for the owners to leave, then licks the ceilings, leaving dark stains.

*4. Chōchinobake* – Chōchinobake are animated paper lanterns, with a single eye and a lolling tongue. Genuine chōchinobake are harmless, though evil ghosts or 'onryō' may use their form as a disguise.

*5. Ryūjin* – The ryū are creatures from Japan that look somewhat like European dragons, though, like the Chinese long, they are usually kindly. Ryūjin is a ryū of the sea that lives in a coral palace below the waves and controls the tides with two magical jewels.

*6. Kuzuryū* – An unusual ryū for Japan, as it was once evil, nine-headed Kuzuryū demanded the sacrifice of young girls. The beast was tamed by a priest and transformed into a protective deity.

*7. Kappa* – An impish river demon, the kappa has a head like a monkey and a turtle shell. It has a dip in its skull containing an elixir, the source of its immense power. It demands to wrestle any traveller who wishes to pass and is extremely fond of cucumbers.

*8. Oni* – Terrifying ogres or demons of enormous strength, Oni usually have blue or red skin, horns and fangs. Oni bring disease and disaster, yet their image is sometimes used on temple roofs to scare away other monsters.

*9. Jinmenju* – The Jinmenju is a tree laden with human-faced fruits. They are capable of speech, but more often sit giggling in their branches. Those that laugh too much fall to the ground where they may be picked up and eaten.

*10. Namazu* – A great catfish that causes earthquakes, Namazu is normally controlled by the god Kashima, who keeps it under a rock. When Kashima is distracted, Namazu rebels, shaking its tail and sending tremors through the earth and sea.

*We have travelled so far for so long, but still the strange messages follow me. As I wrote the log of this visit, my quill came to life in my hand. It began to write of its own accord:*

⊕♁♈  ♒♅  ♓♍♈  
♒○♀  ♄♈♓  ♈♓♀♍♁  
♓♍♄♉  
⊕♁♃♃♃♃♅✳

*I did not write this. It was the quill, which has now disappeared from the ship. It was the Monsters. It was the Yōkai. It was the Yōk—*

## Instructions for defeating a Kappa

Bow deeply. The kappa is extremely polite and will feel compelled to return the courtesy. The magical waters will then spill from its head, diminishing the creature's power.

O=F

I am realising that monsters pay no heed to the boundaries humans create. They cross geographical borders, religions and cultures. Nagas, for example, appear across South and South-East Asia, and can be found in the traditions of the Hindu, Buddhist and Jain religions. — RB

PAKISTAN

NEPAL

BHUTAN

BANGLADESH

LAOS

THAILAND

MYANMAR (BURMA)

INDIA

Bay of Bengal

Arabian Sea

16. Apalala

13. Rakshasa

12. Indian Naga

14. Vetala

11. Chinthe

15. Pishacha

17. Nari Latha Wela

SRI LANKA

*Three of my men were mesmerised by this plant for several days.*

Ψ=B

9. Makara

CHINA

TAIWAN

**1. Pugot**

One sailor was snatched by a foul, stinking pugot. We found him later, terrified but unharmed.

South China Sea

PHILIPPINES

*South and South-East Asia*

**2. Buso**

Busos are very stupid beasts. We heard many tales of how they may be outwitted.

Philippine Sea

**10. Tipaka**

VIETNAM

CAMBODIA

**6. Nagini**

**3. Pontianak**

BRUNEI

**4. Gerjis**

MALAYSIA

**5. Indonesian Naga**

SINGAPORE

INDONESIA

TIMOR LESTE

**7. Leyak**

**8. Barong**

Hal, our cook's boy, kept night watch, ready to fight off marauding leyaks with his cleaver.

Indian Ocean

# South and South-East Asia

We travelled on to warmer climates, seeking new marvels. Great rivers and still lakes reflected the high mountains and green hills of this region. Every place we came to brought fresh stories of monsters.

**1. Pugot** - These stinking, headless monsters of the Philippines haunt deserted buildings. They will chase humans, sometimes sending them insane, but they eat only centipedes and snakes.

**2. Buso** - Ugly ogres of the Philippines, busos have curling hair, enormous mouths, two protruding teeth and one eye. They lurk in graveyard trees, feasting upon the flesh of the dead.

**3. Pontianak** - This horrifying female vampire-ghost stalks the jungles of Malaysia and Indonesia. She feeds on the blood of children.

**4. Gerjis** - Found in Malaysia, the Gerjis was a gigantic tiger that preyed on every creature in the jungle. He was finally defeated by Kancil, the mouse-deer, who tricked him into climbing into a pit to avoid the sky falling on him. The other animals quickly filled the hole.

**5. Indonesian Naga** - These semi-divine serpents take many forms. In Indonesia and Thailand they are dragon-like creatures that guard gates and entrances and they may boast up to seven heads. They also guard treasure.

**6. Nagini** - Nagini are the female form of naga. They are women from the waist up, with the tail of a snake. Incredibly beautiful and holders of great wisdom, they sometimes marry mortal princes. There are stories of naga and nagini throughout South and South-East Asia.

**7. Leyak** - By day, these vampire-like creatures seem like normal humans. At night, however, they seek human entrails to brew an elixir which gives them the power to shape-shift. They take what they need from cemeteries, or even sleeping people. Leyaks can take off their heads to fly through the night. They are found on the island of Bali in Indonesia.

**8. Barong** - This beast has rolling eyes, a lolling tongue and long fangs. Despite its appearance, the Barong is considered a creature of good fortune, as it constantly battles the evil, child-eating witch Rangda. The Barong is also found in Bali.

**9. Makara** - This sea monster, common in the stories of Indonesia, Thailand and India, takes many forms. It often appears with the body parts of elephants and crabs but is usually made up of at least two different creatures, one of the earth and one of the sea.

**10. Tipaka** - A magical winged horse, Tipaka is capable of flying through the heavens. He is so fast, he reaches his destination as soon as his rider sets out. Tipaka was the mount of the great King Sison of Thailand. Sison wielded a magical sword that destroyed his enemies. If he forgot to invoke the correct god, however, the blade would kill his own men.

**11. Chinthe** - These great lion-dogs of Myanmar often have wings and nearly always appear in pairs. They are ferocious, brave and loyal and guard temples and shrines.

**12. Indian Naga** - Indian naga, unlike those in Indonesia and Thailand, are human from the waist up and serpents from the waist down. They live in beautiful palaces, either underwater or underground, and may be of many colours. These creatures can be benevolent or evil.

**13. Rakshasa** - Demons of the Hindu mythology of India, rakshasa may take any form, from beautiful women to foul giants. They are most dangerous at night, especially during the darkness when their strength increases. Most powerful of all was the ten-headed Ravana, their king, who abducted the princess, Sita.

7.

3.

16.

1.

2.

8.

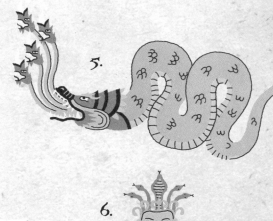
5.

6.

A famous fight between Barong and Rangda is still remembered today by Balinese dancers. In it, Barong casts a spell to protect human warriors against black magic. – RB

Hindu mythology has numerous extraordinary beasts, which turn up in many stories. In the great epic the **Ramayana**, the rakshasa Ravana is defeated by Prince Rama, with the aid of the famous monkey general Hanuman and his army of monkeys. — RB

*14. Vetala* - These demons haunt battlefields in India, seeking new hosts. They inhabit the bodies of their latest victims and if their current body is destroyed, they move on to another.

*15. Pishacha* - Pishachas are creatures from Hindu mythology. They infest cemeteries looking for corpses. Regarded as disease-demons, they also attack the sick, eating them from within.

*16. Apalala* - This ghastly water monster from the Swat River, Pakistan, was once a magician named Gangi. Gangi restrained dragons with special charms but when the local people failed to show him gratitude, he resolved to be reborn as Apalala, the worst of all serpents. Apalala brought storms and floods and devastated crops. He was tamed by the Buddha and now floods the earth once every 12 years, so he may feed.

*17. Nari Latha Wela* - This strange and mysterious vine of Sri Lanka bears a curious flower. It resembles a beautiful woman and has the power to distract humans from prayer. It blooms only once every 20 years.

*Twelve months seemed but hours when studying the wondrous creatures of this region, but at length we began to sense a threatening presence, as with other realms we had visited. After watching the strange antics of the dancing Barong, my eye was drawn to the footsteps it had created in the ground. The swirls in the dirt had formed peculiar shapes:*

*As I copied this, a sudden gust of wind blew over my lantern, shattering the glass and setting fire to my precious maps. I ruined my second-best cloak putting out the blaze.*

The more I study these strange markings, the more I start to see a pattern. At present I cannot say what that might be. — RB

TURKEY

ARMENIA

15. *Karakoncolos*

13. *Ghoul*

SYRIA

Mediterranean Sea

CYPRUS

14. *Kulullû*

16. *Leviathan*

LEBANON

IRAQ

WEST BANK

GAZA ----

ISRAEL

JORDAN

12. *Girtablilî*

EGYPT

We were filled with joy to see this bird!

Here a great stone sphinx can be seen in the desert.

11. *Phoenix*

SAUDI ARABIA

17. *Sphinx*

Red Sea

10. *Unicorn*

SUDAN

The Middle East

ERITREA

ETHIOPIA

AZERBAIJAN   8. *Asdeev*

UZBEKISTAN

TURKMENISTAN

*Caspian Sea*

4. *Manticore*

5. *Huma Bird*

AFGHANISTAN

At night we heard the
dreadful manticore's call.

IRAN

7. *Lamassu*

6. *Simurgh*

1. *Jinn*
Our lamp had a cursed
jinn inside.

The lamassu we saw
appeared to have been
turned to stone.

KUWAIT

PAKISTAN

BAHRAIN

QATAR

UNITED ARAB
EMIRATES

We narrowly escaped death when Hal
spotted the Zaratan's eye through some
trees on the 'island' we had landed on.

9. *Roc*

2. *Zaratan*

OMAN

YEMEN

3. *Dandan*

*Arabian Sea*

# The Middle East

*Onwards we journeyed, deep into the mountains and deserts of the East. The beasts of this region may appear from the eye of a sandstorm, the foam of the waves or even from enchanted lamps. Desert travellers often spend their nights in the relative safety of caravanserai camps.*

**1. Jinn** – Magical spirits of flame and air, jinn were formed, it is said, from a black, smokeless fire thousands of years before humans. They may take human or animal form, or even appear as pillars of swirling smoke. Jinn can be evil or benevolent, but will punish humans that offend them. They are found throughout the folklore of the Middle East.

**2. Zaratan** – This sea turtle is so vast it has mountains, trees and valleys on its back. Sailors land on it, mistaking it for an island, but drown when the creature goes underwater.

**3. Dandan** – A hideous sea monster, spoken of by Arabian sailors, the Dandan can devour a ship and its entire crew in one bite, but is killed if it eats human flesh. An ointment made from its liver allows the user to breathe underwater.

**4. Manticore** – This hideous man-eating beast has a lion's body and a human head. Its tail is fanned with poisoned spines, with which it shoots its prey. Its call sounds like a flute and trumpet played together. It is found in many places, but it originated in Iran and its name comes from the Persian for 'man eater'.

**5. Huma Bird** – The huma bird of Iran ('fabulous bird' in Persian) lives its entire life in the air. It is impossible to catch but brings good fortune and happiness to any who sight it, or even glimpse its shadow. If someone should kill a huma, however, their own death will come within 40 days.

**6. Simurgh** – A most ancient and wise bird, the Simurgh dwells among the Elberz Mountains of Iran. Its multicoloured, magical feathers have healing properties but the bird will sing only for its mate. If captured, it will die.

**7. Lamassu** – Wise, protective spirits of Assyria (a kingdom of ancient Mesopotamia), lamassu have the bodies of lions, the wings of eagles and the heads of wise men. They may be seen at the gates of great cities and palaces, poised to battle chaos and evil.

7.

Statues of lamassu guarded the palace of Nineveh, part of the Assyrian Empire, in ancient Mesopotamia. The Mesopotamian civilisation flourished around the Tigris and Euphrates Rivers in Syria, Iran, Iraq and Turkey around 3000–500BC. Perhaps these statues are the lamassu "turned to stone" that Walters mentions on the map? Girtablili and kulullû are also creatures from ancient Mesopotamian tradition. — RB

12.

11.

17.

4.

9.

## Instructions for defeating a Karakoncolos

*If the Karakoncolos tricks his way into the house, you can trick him by setting fire to some silk. In reply he will set alight his own fur, then run into the street in terror.*

15.

6.

13.

**8. Asdeev** - Asdeev was a white, fire-belching dragon, found in Iran. It was said to be a 'dev', or demonic giant, turned by magic into a great serpent. It was killed by the Persian hero, Rustem.

**9. Roc** - The mightiest of all birds, the Roc is so huge it can grab an elephant in its talons, dash it against a rock and then carry the corpse to its nest to be gobbled up by its young. It may be seen circling the skies above the Arabian Peninsula.

**10. Unicorn** - Unicorns are to be found in many countries, in many forms. Most are recognisable by their grace, wisdom and the single horn on their heads. I saw one in the deserts of Arabia.

**11. Phoenix** - The firebird has great beauty and elegance, with brilliant rainbow plumage. At 500 years of age it is consumed by a fire of spices, and reborn from the ashes. There are accounts of the phoenix throughout the Middle East, Asia and Europe.

**12. Girtablili** - Fearsome creatures, half-human, half-scorpion, girtablili are as tall as the sky itself. They guard entrances for the goddess Tiamat. One look from them means death.

**13. Ghoul** - A demonic form of jinn that preys on travellers in deserts, forests and the wilderness, ghouls also haunt battlefields and cemeteries where they devour corpses from graves. They are feared throughout the Middle East.

**14. Kulullû** - Half-human, half-fish, the kulullû are water spirits. They are thought to bring protection to households. In the Assyrian culture of ancient Mesopotamia, people sometimes hid images of them in their homes.

**15. Karakoncolos** - This ugly bogeyman lurks on street corners setting riddles to passers-by. Those who answer incorrectly are struck dead. He is found in Turkey and also Bulgaria, Serbia and Greece.

**16. Leviathan** - A twisted, coiling sea serpent, the Leviathan is more than 900 miles in length. It can consume dragons.

**17. Sphinx** - Sphinxes appear in many forms. Most sphinxes have the body of a lion, yet depending on the region in which they live, they may have the heads of humans, rams, falcons or even pharaohs. Some are winged. The ancient Egyptians made many statues of sphinxes.

*As we crossed barren desert, the howling of distant beasts brought terror to our company. Turning for one final glance at the dunes below us, we were astonished to see, etched into the sands, this strange and disturbing pattern:*

⊗⊙ ⵠ⚇⊙
⊗ⵠⵙ⵩⅄⚇ⵜ⵶⚹
⵶ⵏⵚ⚲

I find myself beginning to wonder if there is some truth in Walters' ravings. Clearly I need fewer late nights! — RB

From his illustration, it is possible that Walters sighted an Arabian oryx (a type of antelope) and mistook it for the mythical unicorn. He would not be the first! — RB

## The Tale of the Fisherman and the Jinn

*In the bazaars they tell of a magical bottle inhabited by a jinn. When a poor fisherman caught the bottle in his net, he accidentally released the jinn, who wanted to kill him. The fisherman tricked the jinn into getting back into the bottle, but the trapped spirit promised it would make the fisherman rich if he set it free.*

*The jinn led the fisherman to a magic pool where he caught four fish so beautiful he took them to the sultan. The sultan commanded that they be cooked but as each fish fried, strange things happened. A person would appear through the wall, talk with the fish, then burn it to ashes. Mystified, the sultan went to the lake and found a prince, half-turned to stone by an evil sorceress. The sultan released the man, helped him gain revenge and they became friends.*

*The fisherman was richly rewarded by the sultan.*

'The Fisherman and the Jinn', which Walters tells here, can be found in the **Thousand and One Nights.** This famous collection of tales was written down in Arabic sometime between the 9th and 13th centuries, but the stories come from many cultures from across the Middle East and Asia. — RB

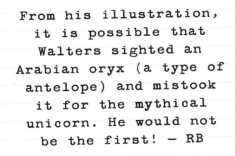

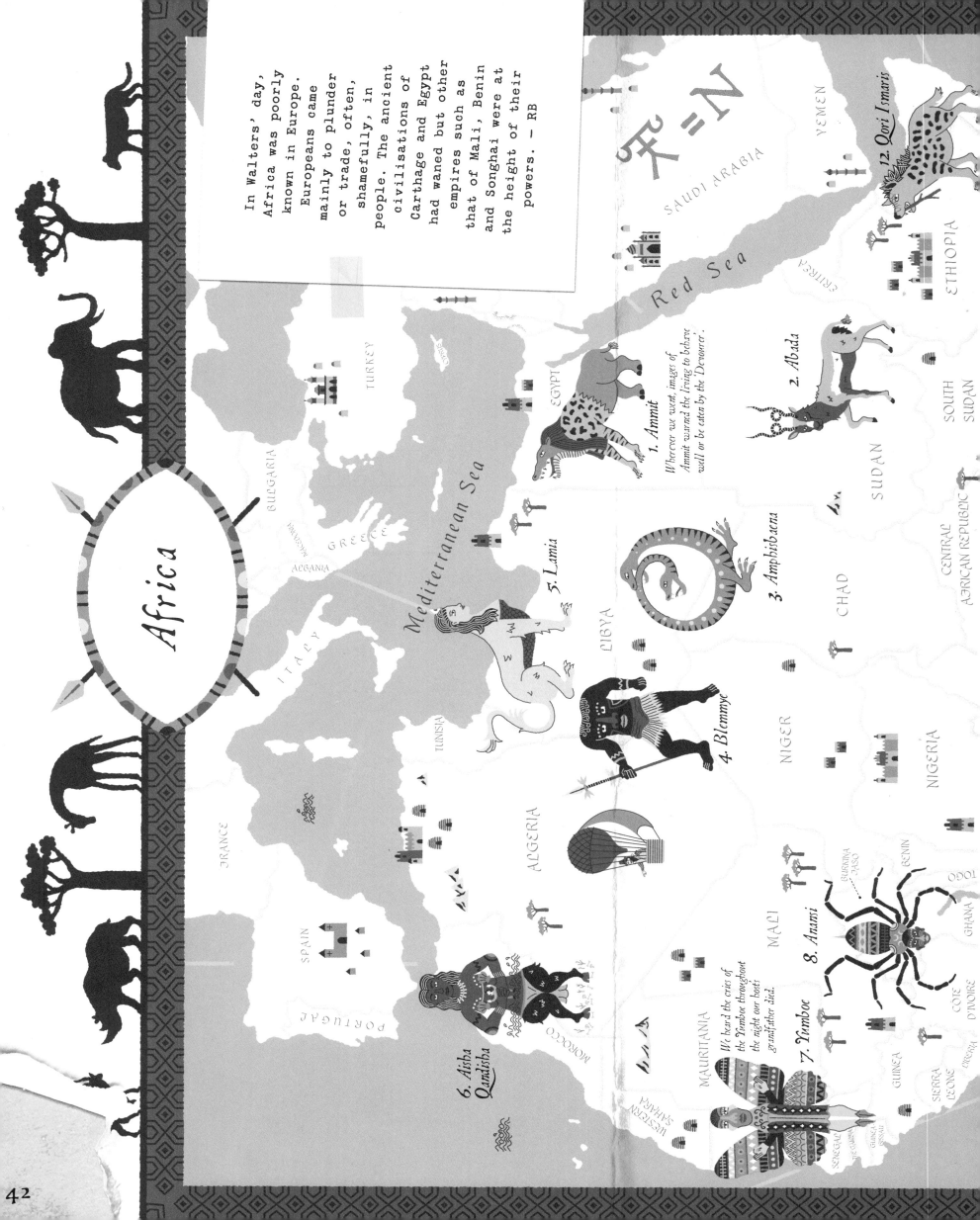

# Africa

In Walters' day, Africa was poorly known in Europe. Europeans came mainly to plunder or trade, often, shamefully, in people. The ancient civilisations of Carthage and Egypt had waned but other empires such as that of Mali, Benin and Songhai were at the height of their powers. – RB

Red Sea

Mediterranean Sea

SAUDI ARABIA

YEMEN

TURKEY

CYPRUS

EGYPT

ERITREA

ETHIOPIA

SOUTH SUDAN

SUDAN

BULGARIA

MACEDONIA

GREECE

ALBANIA

ITALY

CHAD

LIBYA

CENTRAL AFRICAN REPUBLIC

NIGER

TUNISIA

NIGERIA

BENIN

TOGO

GHANA

ALGERIA

MALI

BURKINA FASO

CÔTE D'IVOIRE

GUINEA

SIERRA LEONE

FRANCE

SPAIN

PORTUGAL

MOROCCO

MAURITANIA

WESTERN SAHARA

SENEGAL

GUINEA BISSAU

THE GAMBIA

1. Ammit

*Wherever we went, images of Ammit warned the living to behave well or be eaten by the 'Devourer'.*

2. Abada

3. Amphisbaena

4. Blemmye

5. Lamia

6. Aisha Qandisha

7. Yumboe

*We heard the cries of the Yumboe throughout the night our hosts grandfather died.*

8. Anansi

12. Qori Ismaris

42

SOMALIA

KENYA

UGANDA

RWANDA

BURUNDI

TANZANIA

11. Biloko

10. Emela-ntouka

CAMEROON

GABON

REPUBLIC OF THE CONGO

EQUATORIAL GUINEA

SAO TOME AND PRINCIPE

DEMOCRATIC REPUBLIC OF THE CONGO

ANGOLA

13. Nyaminyami

*Although generally protective, Nyaminyami can cause tremors and earthquakes.*

ZAMBIA

MALAWI

MOZAMBIQUE

COMOROS

MADAGASCAR

15. Na-te-reo

*We lost Rogers to this demonic plant. He was a good man and a fine ship's carpenter.*

Indian Ocean

19. Inkanyamba

16. Grootslang

14. Tokoloshe

ZIMBABWE

SWAZILAND

LESOTHO

BOTSWANA

NAMIBIA

SOUTH AFRICA

17. Impundulu

*There were fearsome storms in this area and we knew the lightning bird was near.*

18. Abatwa

9. Fengu

*We were keen to encounter a fengu, for they bring good luck, cure from illness and fair weather. As Hal said, we needed all of these!*

Atlantic Ocean

H = C

43

# Africa

We journeyed on, joining a camel train across the Sahara Desert. The beasts discovered in Africa are fascinating and strange. Some are supremely dangerous, others more kindly.

*1. Ammit* - Part-lion, part-hippopotamus, part-crocodile, Ammit was a female demon feared by ancient Egyptians as the 'Soul-Eater' or 'Devourer'. If a corpse's heart is weighed against a feather and found unworthy, it is consumed by Ammit, leaving the deceased person's soul to eternal unrest.

*2. Abada* - These creatures are similar to unicorns, but have two crooked horns. They are usually seen in north-east Africa.

*3. Amphisbaena* - This two-headed serpent of the desert has the legs and claws of an eagle and a venomous bite. It hatches its eggs in sand dunes and, if cut in half, will join its body back together. It is said to inhabit Libya and I have read that its skin, when dried, cures a cold.

*4. Blemmye* - A tribe of headless humans, Blemmyes have their faces on their chests. Though we saw many images of Blemmyes on maps of Libya, we did not witness a single one.

*5. Lamia* - Queen of Libya, Lamia was turned into a hideous, child-eating monster by a jealous goddess. She has the head and body of a woman but the tail of a snake. Lamia takes out her eyes at night to keep watch while she sleeps.

*6. Aisha Qandisha* - This female river demon appears as a beautiful woman. Men she ensnares fail to notice her feet, which are those of a camel or goat. She appears in the folklore of Morocco.

*7. Yumboe* - Mischievous but not malevolent, these fairies steal food and drink from villages. They become very attached to certain households, and can be heard wailing with grief when a family member dies. Yumboes can be found on Gorée Island, Senegal.

*8. Anansi* - A spider who is both wise and a trickster, Anansi is the keeper of the world's stories and spins them like webs for all to enjoy. Stories of Anansi were first told in Ghana and his fame spread throughout West Africa.

*9. Jengu* - These beautiful water spirits of Cameroon have wild hair and fish tails and they bring good luck, fair weather and protection from disease to those that honour them. They also serve as messengers between humans and the gods.

*10. Emela-ntouka* - A violent swamp monster, Emela-ntouka's name means 'killer of elephants' in the Lingala language of the Congo. It has a tail like a crocodile and a single, deadly horn.

*11. Biloko* - These dwarf-like creatures have sharp claws and teeth, are clothed entirely in leaves and smell of rotting vegetables. They carry bells through the rainforests, lulling their victims to sleep. By morning the sleepers are reduced to bones.

*12. Qori Ismaris* - This evil sorcerer turns into a hyena at night by rubbing his body with a magical stick. At dawn, he returns to his human form by the same method. He is found in Somalia.

*13. Nyaminyami* - Nyaminyami is a spirit of the Zambezi River, Zimbabwe. He appears in the form of a serpent, with the head of a fish. He has been separated from his wife by a dam, which makes him angry from time to time.

*14. Tokoloshe* - Dwarf zombies of southern Africa, tokoloshe appear in many forms but are usually covered in fur, are foul-smelling and have glowing eyes. They bite the toes off people as they sleep. They are clearly visible to children and have a magic pebble that they use to become invisible.

*15. Ya-te-veo* - An appalling, human-eating tree of Madagascar, the Ya-te-veo may be distinguished by thick, fleshy leaves and long, drooping tendrils. It snatches its victims and drinks their blood.

*16. Grootslang* - This gigantic beast lives in the Bottomless Pit, a cave somewhere in the mountains of north-east South Africa. It takes the shape of an elephant with a snake's tail. The Grootslang guards a priceless treasure of diamonds, and will devour all that seek it.

*17. Impundulu* - The feared impundulu, or lightning bird, causes storms by beating its wings. It lives on blood and enjoys inflicting pain. It is said a lone impundulu can devastate an entire herd of cattle in a single night. It spreads disease and can kill humans. This creature is found in stories of the Zulu and Xhosa peoples of South Africa.

Walters would have read about Lamia, Blemmyes and the amphisbaena serpent in **Naturalis Historia** (Natural History) by the Roman author Pliny the Elder. Pliny was not well-travelled and relied on other people's descriptions of distant creatures. Some were undoubtedly tall tales. — RB

17.

12.

1.

As people have travelled around the world, their creatures have moved with them. Stories of Anansi have reached as far as the Caribbean and North and South America.

19.

10.

11.

18.

9.

4.

**18. Abatwa** - These tiny creatures are found in the mythology of the Zulu people of South Africa. They are like humans in miniature and they ride on and farm ants. They are peaceful, but if accidentally stepped on, will push a sharp barb into the offending foot.

**19. Inkanyamba** - This enormous, serpentine water monster of South Africa is responsible for whirlpools and tornados. The inkanyamba grows to an enormous size as it curls out of its underwater lair and then shrinks at it re-enters, causing perilous waterspouts.

*Still grieving the mortal loss of Rogers, our carpenter, to the Ya-te-veo, we were glad to leave this continent, yet the vast body of water before us filled our hearts with dread. Local fishermen warned us to turn back, but my crew were determined. As we set sail, a great shoal of fish swam before us, forming a strange pattern:*

## The Tale of how Anansi got his Legs

*Anansi loved to eat but he was very lazy. One day Rabbit was cooking and invited his friend to dinner. Anansi didn't want to help cook, so he attached some web-silk to one of his legs and told Rabbit to pull it when the food was ready. He went to visit other animals and they all invited him to eat. Soon greedy Anansi had silks tied to each of his eight legs.*

*When the food was ready the animals all tugged – at the same moment! Poor Anansi was pulled in eight directions. He leapt into the river to melt the silks but his legs had been stretched, which is why spiders' legs are so skinny today.*

16.

6.

2.

5.

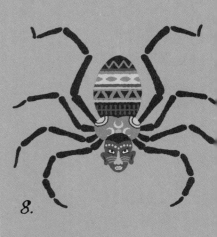

8.

It is perfectly natural for fish to swim in schools, so why am I beginning to believe Cornelius is reporting what he saw? Perhaps it has something to do with the strange pattern my pens formed when I dropped a pencil case yesterday. It looked just like Walters' message . . . I barely dare write this down! — RB

21. Kushtaka

Alaska
(United States)

20. Amarok

Bering Sea

Gulf of Alaska

CANADA

23. Tizheruk

22. Haietlik
The people of these parts draw
pictograms of the Haietlik. It is not
believed to be dangerous.

10. Sasquatch
Local people showed us
gigantic footprints left
by this creature.

North
Pacific
Ocean

North
America

9. Jackalope

7. Haakapainiži

Hawaii
(United States)

6. Ahuízotl

5. Chupacabra

46

**19. Nulayuuiniq**

The boulder that was once Nulayuuiniq can still be seen.

**18. Miqqiayuuq**

Making offerings to the Mishepishu will help travellers cross the water safely.

**14. Mishepishu**

**13. Squonk**

**15. Stone Giants**

At Hal's suggestion, we escaped these giants by climbing a tree – they cannot look up.

*Greenland (Denmark)*

**17. Erqigdlit**

*Davis Strait*

*Labrador Sea*

**16. Auvekoejak**

One of my men fell in love with an Auvekoejak mer-woman.

*Hudson Bay*

UNITED
STATES
OF
AMERICA

**12. Jersey Devil**

**11. Piasa Bird**

**8. Plat-Eye**

*North Atlantic Ocean*

MEXICO

*Gulf of Mexico*

**2. Zombie**

We trod carefully, for anyone in this land might be a zombie in disguise.

BAHAMAS

**1. Legarou**

CUBA

JAMAICA    HAITI

Puerto Rico (United States)

DOMINICAN
REPUBLIC

ANTIGUA AND BARBUDA

Guadeloupe (France)

DOMINICA

ST KITTS AND NEVIS

Martinique (France)

ST LUCIA

ST VINCENT
AND THE
GRENADINES

BARBADOS

GRENADA

TRINIDAD AND TOBAGO

**4. Maya Cosmic Crocodile**

GUATEMALA    HONDURAS

EL SALVADOR    NICARAGUA

**3. La Cegua**

*Caribbean Sea*

PANAMA

COSTA RICA

COLOMBIA

VENEZUELA

# North America

The voyage to these lands took many weeks and, after Roger's disappearance, the crew were uneasy. This continent has every kind of landscape: vast expanses of snow, grassy plains, towering mountains, dark forests, deep lakes and deserts. Each of these terrains is home to curious creatures.

**1. Legarou** - These wicked sorcerers of the Caribbean can transform themselves into animals, trees or objects. It is hard to recognise a legarou, for they take many forms. Some suck blood from between the toes of sleeping victims.

**2. Zombie** - Common in the stories of Haiti, a zombie is one whose body has been brought back from the dead. It is said many who walk these lands are the slaves of the sorcerers that have reanimated them after death.

**3. La Cegua** - A terrifying witch found in the forests of Nicaragua, La Cegua appears at first to be a beautiful woman, then sheds her skin to reveal the features of a horse. Even her whisper will drive those who hear it insane.

**4. Maya Cosmic Crocodile** - The 'starry deer crocodile' holds up the heavens and was a symbol of power for the Maya kings of Mesoamerica (the region from central Mexico south to El Salvador). It has two heads, one of a crocodile with the ears of a deer, the other hangs upside down.

**5. Chupacabra** - Found in Mexico, this reptilian creature is the size of a bear and has a row of sharp spikes down its back. Called 'the goat sucker', it drains blood from its victims like a vampire.

**6. Ahuizotl** - The Ahuizotl is a Mexican water monster from Aztec legend. It has a human hand on the end of its tail. It uses the hand to pull victims into the water, where it dines on their eyeballs, teeth and nails.

**7. Haakapainiži** - This giant grasshopper has spiked legs and a basket on his back to store the children he catches for his supper. He is from California in the United States.

**8. Plat-eye** - Plat-eyes are the spirits of those who have not received a proper burial. Tales of plat-eyes are common in the states of Georgia and South Carolina in the United States.

**9. Jackalope** - Jackalopes are jackrabbits with antlers like those of a deer. Called 'warrior rabbits' by some, they use their antlers to fight and can move at lightning speed. They are found in the western United States.

**10. Sasquatch** - A gigantic wild man covered in shaggy hair, the Sasquatch walks upright, leaving huge footprints. It can grow larger than two tall humans and is found between the Pacific North-West and Alaska.

**11. Piasa Bird** - This terrifying bird-monster has the head and beard of a man, the horns of a deer, the wings of an eagle and the scales and tail of a fish.

**12. Jersey Devil** - A jersey devil is a monster from the state of New Jersey in the United States. It has the wings of a bat, a serpent's tail, hairy legs like a goat, a horse's head, a human body and talons.

**13. Squonk** - The ugliest, saddest creature in the world, the squonk has scaly skin, covered in warts. It is easy to track this lonely beast as it hides in the forest, lamenting its ugly appearance; just listen for loud sobbing. On capture, the creature dissolves into a puddle of tears. It is usually seen in the state of Pennsylvania.

**14. Mishepishu** - This water monster, whose name means 'the great lynx', has a cat-like face and scales. Copper may be harvested from its horns, but the creature's permission must be obtained. It is found in North America's Great Lakes.

**15. Stone Giants** - Also known as 'stone-coats', this ancient race of giants from the legends of the Iroquois Indians wear clothing made of rock. The giants are dangerous to humans but their armour prevents them from running or looking up.

Haakapainiži is found in American Indian folklore in California. The Kawaiisu call him 'Haakapainiži'. The Chemehuevi call him 'Aatakapitsi'. — RB

A rock painting of the Piasa Bird may be found near Alton, Illinois, above the Mississippi River. The creature's name means 'devourer of humans' in the language of the Illinois Indians. — RB

**16. Auvekoejak** - The Auvekoejak are mer-folk of Greenland. Part-human, part-fish, they have tails of fur instead of scales to protect them from the cold.

**17. Erqigdlit** - These blood drinking monsters have the top halves of humans and the hindquarters of dogs. They are from the Inuit traditions of Greenland and Canada (where they are called 'adlet').

**18. Miqqiayuuq** - This shaggy, hair-covered monster is found in the stories of the Inuit people of Hudson Bay in Canada. It lurks beneath ice, waiting for people to lower their buckets into the water, then tangles the ropes so they get nothing.

**19. Nulayuuiniq** - The Nulayuuiniq was a baby born in a time of great famine. When people from a nearby village brought food, they found this infant grown to a giant size, having eaten everyone in her village. She chased her rescuers too but, growing weary, she rested and turned to stone. The Nulayuuiniq is also from Hudson Bay, Canada.

**20. Amarok** - This immense wolf bites off the heads of its victims. It is found in the stories of the Inuit people of Alaska and Canada.

**21. Kushtaka** - Shape shifting otter-humans, kushtaka steal their victims' spirits and turn them, too, into kushtaka. They appear in the legends of the Tlingit and Tsimshian Indians of Alaska and Canada.

**22. Haietlik** - This creature has the body of a long alligator and the head of a horse. If a fisherman is lucky enough to carry the skin of this creature in his boat, he may catch a whale. From Nootka Indian folklore.

**23. Tizheruk** - Also from the legends of the Inuit people, Tizheruk is a serpent-like sea monster with a fish tail and terrible claws, with which it snatches fishermen.

In Greenland, my crew was further depleted by the loss of Job Merryweather, who stayed behind to marry one of the Auvekoejak mer-folk. As we bid one another farewell, Job's new wife presented me with an amulet. I reproduce here its curious engraving:

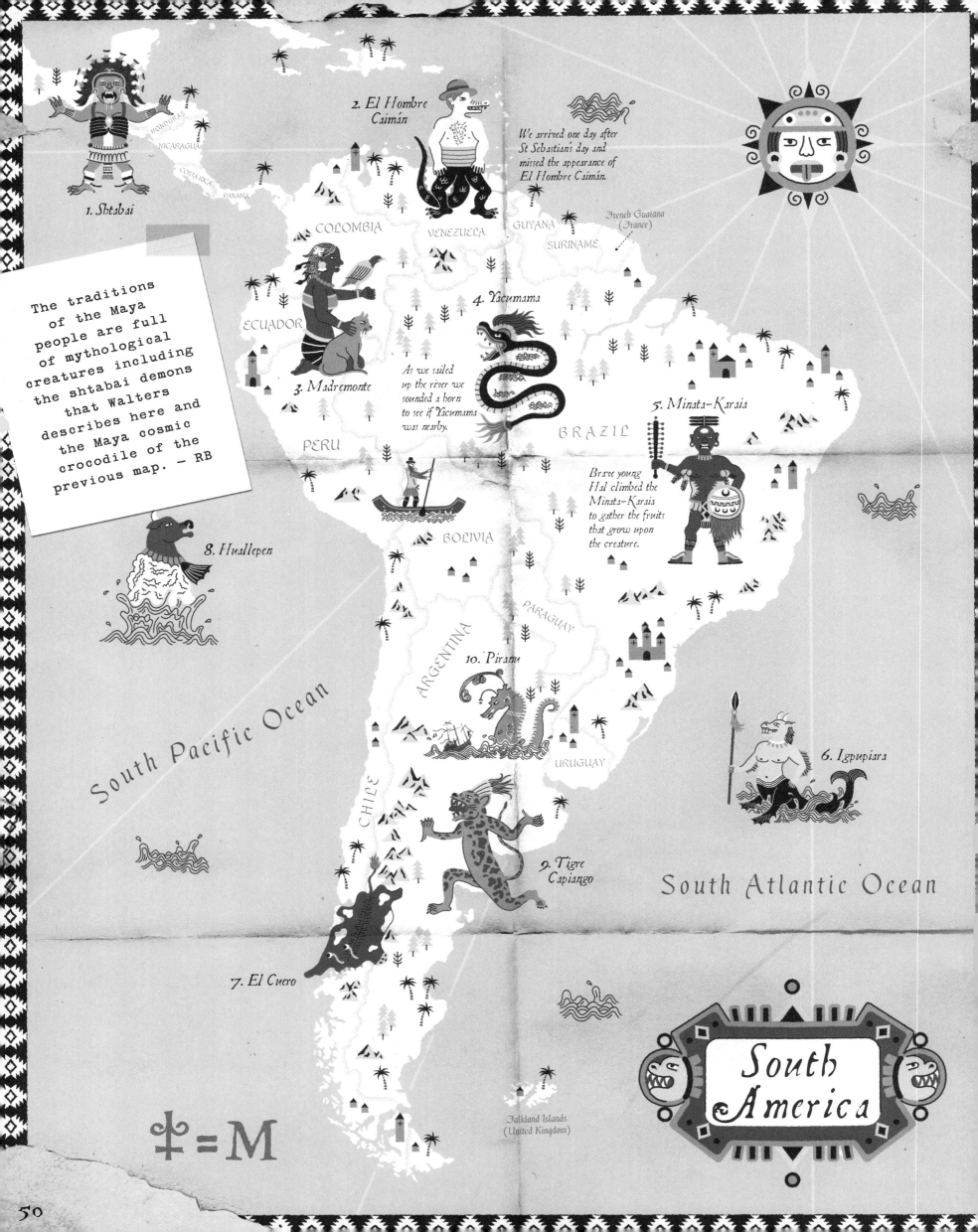

1. Shtabai

2. El Hombre Caimán

We arrived one day after St Sebastian's day and missed the appearance of El Hombre Caimán.

HONDURAS
NICARAGUA
COSTA RICA
PANAMA

COLOMBIA

VENEZUELA

GUYANA

SURINAME

French Guaiana
(France)

ECUADOR

3. Madremonte

4. Yacumama

As we sailed up the river we sounded a horn to see if Yacumama was nearby.

PERU

5. Minata-Karaia

BRAZIL

Brave young Hal climbed the Minata-Karaia to gather the fruits that grow upon the creature.

The traditions of the Maya people are full of mythological creatures including the shtabai demons that Walters describes here and the Maya cosmic crocodile of the previous map. — RB

8. Huallepen

BOLIVIA

PARAGUAY

ARGENTINA

10. Piranu

URUGUAY

6. Igpupiara

South Pacific Ocean

CHILE

9. Tigre Capiango

South Atlantic Ocean

7. El Cuero

⚲ = M

Falkland Islands
(United Kingdom)

South America

50

# South America

As we fought our way through the dense rainforests of South America, we encountered creatures from the tiniest poison frogs to the much more terrifying beasts I describe here. We travelled further south and passed a great range of mountains. The beasts of this continent were some of the strangest we have yet encountered.

**1. Shtabai** – These demons are common in the myths of the Maya people of Mesoamerica. They live in caves and may transform themselves, taking on human appearance.

**2. El Hombre Caimán** – Half-man, half-alligator, El Hombre Caimán (alligator man) was once a fisherman of Colombia who was tricked into losing his human form. Once a year, at the feast day of St Sebastian, the alligator man appears, hunting for human prey.

**3. Madremonte** – This raging spirit of Mother Mountain fiercely protects her lands and creatures. Dressed in moss and leaves, she has eyes of fire, sharp fangs and a consuming anger for any that would defile her natural world. She is found in Colombia.

**4. Yacumama** – This gigantic water snake and guardian of the Amazon River has terrifying, glowing eyes and multicoloured skin. Yacumama sometimes disguises itself as a *supaylancha*, or 'spirit-boat'. It sucks humans and boats into its vast mouth.

**5. Minata-Karaia** – Monstrous giants, as tall as the jungle canopy, Minata-Karaia stride around the rainforests of Brazil. The males have strange holes in their heads that whistle as they move. Delicious fruits, like coconuts, grow from their armpits and they crack them open on their heads to eat them.

**6. Igpupiara** – Igpupiara are mer-people with seal heads, human bodies and fish tails. They prowl the waters around Brazil, luring humans to their lairs.

**7. El Cuero** – This giant, blood-sucking cow hide floats on rivers throughout Chile. Its victims will notice eyes on stalks watching them just before it attacks. It strikes like lightning, folding itself around passers-by and sucking clean their bones. When basking on the river bank it looks like a harmless animal skin laid out to dry in the sun.

**8. Huallepen** – A horrific creature with the head of a calf, the body of a sheep and fin-like flippers, the huallepen lives in remote ponds and rivers in Chile.

**9. Tigre Capiango** – This monster is not unlike the European werewolf, but it takes the form of a jaguar. Sorcerers transform themselves into these creatures by wearing the skins of great cats and chanting incantations. Tigres Capiango prowl through central Argentina.

**10. Piranu** – A monstrous, horse-headed fish with bulging eyes, the Piranu lurks in the rivers of central Argentina. It rams against boats, drowning the sailors inside.

*We slashed through the jungle with sword and scythe to escape a particularly vicious Tigre Capiango. We got away, but as the rainforest closed around us, the creepers tangled and knotted, forming the unearthly patterns I have come to dread:*

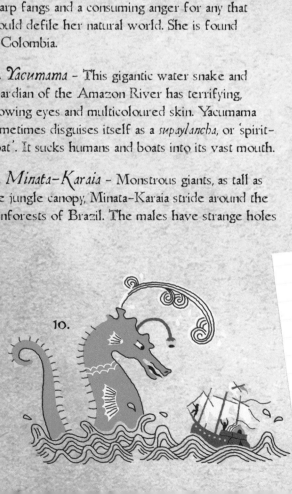

I am trying to to translate this script, but so far with no success. Yesterday I also received a message. I saw letters like this form in the leaves at the bottom of my teacup. I now know Walters was telling the truth. – RB

Of all the beasts in this atlas should we fear Madremonte most of all? – RB

51

⊕ = K

Timor Sea

Arafura Sea

Gulf of
Carpentaria

13. Namorodo

10. Giant Dingo

14. Yara-ma-
yha-who

AUSTRALIA

On being chased by this serpent, I
was instructed to switch direction
quickly. The snake rolled past
and I narrowly escaped.

12. Hoop
Snake

15. Bunyip

11. Muldjewangk

*A Bunyip mother will create a flood to
retrieve her young if they are abducted.*

Great Australian Bight

16. Ningen

*Australia and
New Zealand*

Some have called the Ningen a hoax, as it was first
reported in the 1960s in the Antarctic Ocean.
Here Walters describes it four centuries earlier.
Perhaps it is not a fake after all? — RB

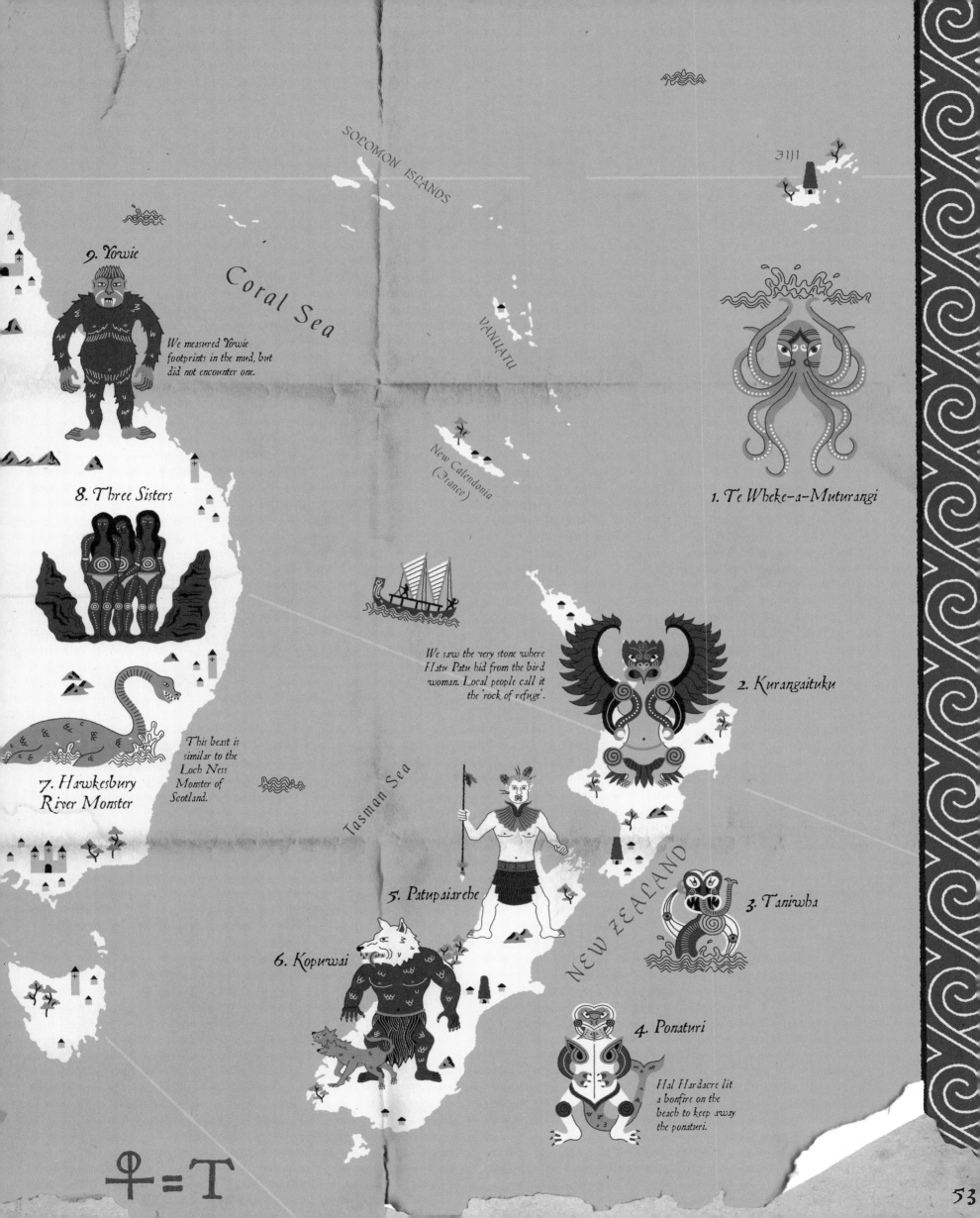

SOLOMON ISLANDS

VANUATU

FIJI

Coral Sea

**9. Yowie**

We measured Yowie footprints in the mud, but did not encounter one.

New Caledonia (France)

**1. Te Wheke-a-Muturangi**

**8. Three Sisters**

We saw the very stone where Hatu Patu hid from the bird woman. Local people call it the 'rock of refuge'.

**2. Kurangaituku**

This beast is similar to the Loch Ness Monster of Scotland.

**7. Hawkesbury River Monster**

Tasman Sea

NEW ZEALAND

**5. Patupaiarehe**

**3. Taniwha**

**6. Kopuwai**

**4. Ponaturi**

Hal Hardacre lit a bonfire on the beach to keep away the ponaturi.

⚥ = T

53

## The Tale of Hatu Patu

The bird woman, Kurangaituku lived in the central North Island and kept small creatures as pets. She also kidnapped a boy called Hatu Patu and kept him prisoner. While she was out hunting, Hatu Patu escaped but one of her pets, a tiny grey warbler, a riroriro, flew to warn the bird woman. She chased Hatu Patu through the steaming springs of Whakarewarewa, into the hottest pool and was boiled to death.

Kurangaituku, like all the creatures Walters mentions in New Zealand, appears in traditional Māori legends. — RB

# Australia and New Zealand

*On we pressed, to the very bottom of the world; further, I believe, than anyone from Europe has ever travelled. We searched for the legendary Terra Australis Incognita, but instead found inhabited lands, unlike any I have seen. Great red rocks, blue mountains and burning deserts on the continent and, on the islands over the sea, strange spouts of boiling water, snow-capped mountains and dense forests.*

**1. Te Wheke-a-Muturangi** - The explorer-hero Kupe left Hawaiki (the mythological homeland of the Polynesian peoples) to chase the giant octopus Te Wheke-a-Muturangi across the ocean after she and her children stole fish from the villager's lines. He followed her so far that he discovered Aotearoa (New Zealand).

**2. Kurangaituku** - This winged ogress has the head of a woman and the claws of a bird.

**3. Taniwha** - This species is found throughout the mythology of the Māori people of New Zealand. The creatures have lizard-like bodies and spiny tails.

Before western explorers travelled this far, map makers used to invent the parts of the globe they didn't know. **Terra Australis Incognita** (unknown southern land) was thought to be a huge southern continent that would balance the world. It seems incredible that Walters came so far — it would have been an extraordinary feat of navigation — yet now I am certain his account is true. — RB

They can devour a human with their mighty fangs, but individual creatures may be befriended. A taniwha called Tuhirangi guided the famous explorer, Kupe, on his travels. Another, Ngake, created the great harbour at the end of the North Island (Te Whanganui-a-Tara or Wellington Harbour) when he crashed through the land to escape to the sea. His brother, Whātaitai, became stranded when he tried to follow. Whātaitai eventually turned to stone.

**4. Ponaturi** - These spirits live in the oceans around New Zealand and have red hair, deadly claws and greenish-white skin that glows in the dark. They fear the sun's fiery light so come ashore only at night.

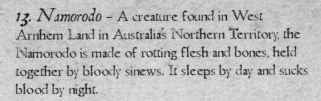

**5. *Patupaiarehe*** - This race of forest-dwelling spirits, usually blond or red-headed, are found throughout New Zealand. Beware them at twilight, for they will lure away any human who has offended them and take them prisoner. Patupaiarehe will occasionally help humans, but wise travellers learn chants to repel the creatures.

**6. *Kopuwai*** - The terrifying giant, Kopuwai, had a pack of two-headed hunting dogs. He kept a woman called Kaiamio as a slave but was killed by warriors from Kaiamio's village and turned to stone. This mountain (also known as 'old man's rock') stands in New Zealand's South Island.

**7. *Hawkesbury River Monster*** - This great serpent lives in the bends of the Hawkesbury River in the state of New South Wales in Australia. It has a long, snake-like neck, tail flippers and scaly skin.

**8. *Three Sisters*** - These rock formations in Australia's Blue Mountains were once young women. They were turned to stone to protect them from a bunyip.

**9. *Yowie*** - An ape-like creature of Australia; some say the yowie is a wild man. It is rarely sighted but occasionally leaves huge footprints.

**10. *Giant Dingo*** - This enormous, carnivorous monster is found in the stories of the Aboriginal people of Cape York Peninsula, Australia. Along with a hideous snake, the dingo terrorised the region. Two brave bird people, the robin and the wagtail, lit a fire and killed them.

**11. *Muldjewangk*** - Half-human, half-fish, these water-folk hide in large lumps of floating seaweed. They live in the Murray River in South Australia.

**12. *Hoop Snake*** - This poisonous snake pursues its victims by holding its tail in its mouth and rolling like a wheel. Stories of this snake are told in Australia and other parts of the world where snakes are common, including the United States.

**13. *Namorodo*** - A creature found in West Arnhem Land in Australia's Northern Territory, the Namorodo is made of rotting flesh and bones, held together by bloody sinews. It sleeps by day and sucks blood by night.

**14. *Yara-ma-yha-who*** - A yara-ma-yha-who can swallow a human whole. They hide in fig trees, then pounce, using suckers on their hands and feet to drain their victims' blood. They swallow their prey, then go to sleep. Upon awakening they regurgitate the human, who comes out smaller and redder and eventually becomes another yara-ma-yha-who.

**15. *Bunyip*** - This abominable, man-eating monster lurks around swamps and billabongs throughout Australia. It may be feathered or furry and have flippers, horse's hooves or the head of an emu, with razor-sharp teeth. Some have tusks, like a walrus. Bunyips threaten people by causing floods and droughts, then enslave their victims before eventually devouring them.

**16. *Ningen*** - Found far south of Australia and New Zealand, near Antarctica, the Ningen is an enormous, blubbery monster whose wobbly, white shape is similar to that of a human. It has two holes for eyes and a slit for a mouth but no other features.

*We are pursued by I know not what. The vastness of these lands strikes fear into our bellies, yet the endless ocean ahead promises little relief. Even as we set sail for territories new, signs painted across the mountains, too high for the hand of a human, appeared before me:*

⚥⚇⚥⚉◦⸸ ⚥⚉◦⸸ ⹖⚶⚸⸸
⸸⚇◦⸸⚥ ⚻⚉⚇⚥⚤⚇⊙
⚥⚻ ⚥⸸⚤⚥ ⚤⚇⚸⚤

## The Tale of the Three Sisters

Three sisters, Meehni, Wimlah and Gunnedoo, were pursued by a hungry bunyip. Their father, Tyawan, hid the girls by turning them to mountains with a magic bone. The bunyip chased Tyawan instead, so he changed himself into a lyrebird, accidentally dropping the bone. Still a bird, he has been searching for the bone ever since so he can return his daughters to human form. The sisters can still be seen as rock formations in the Blue Mountains of south-east Australia.

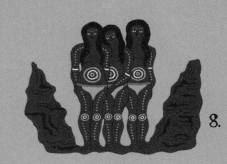

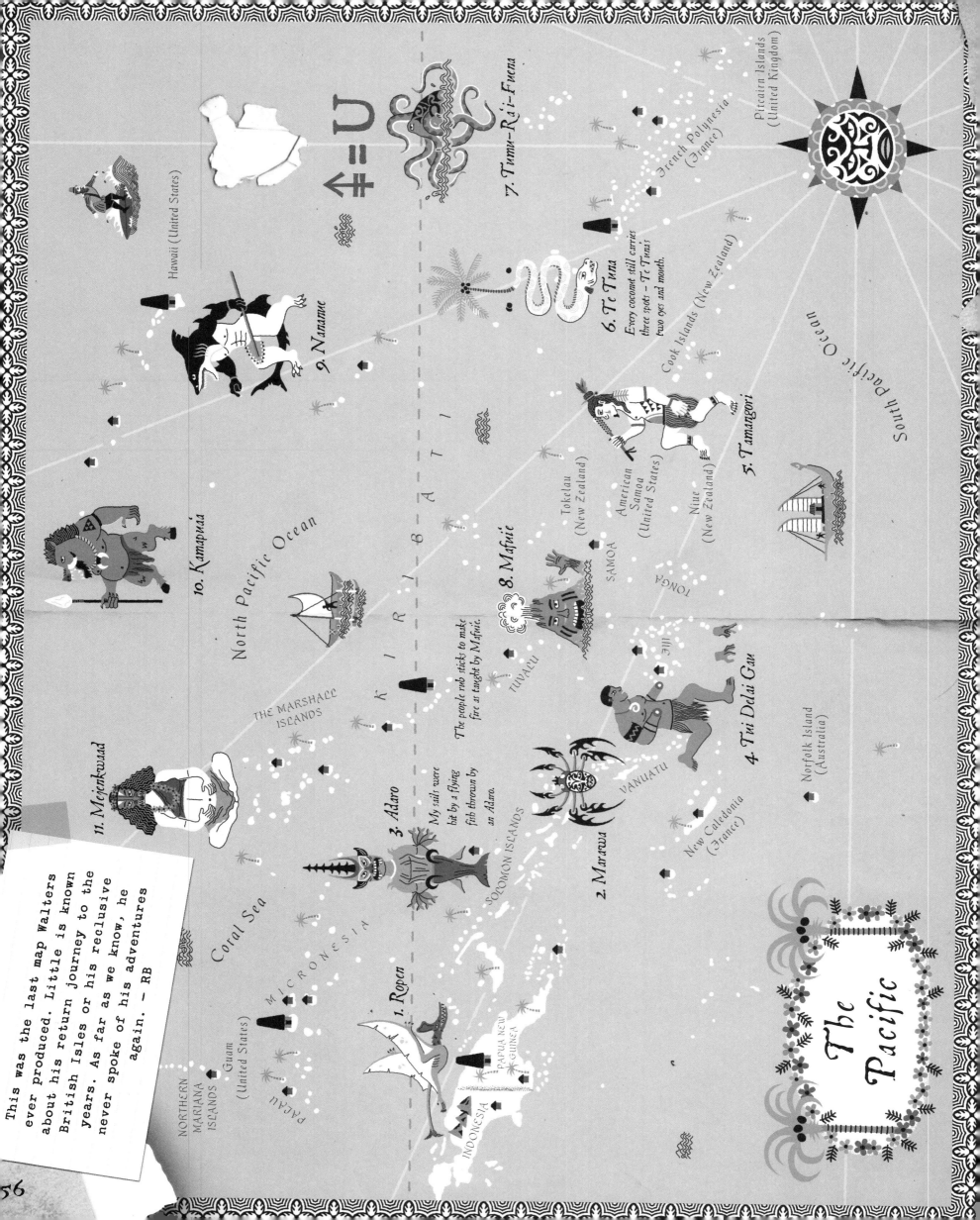

The Pacific

# The Pacific

The bright skies and golden sands of these islands bewitched my crew. My own eyes were drawn to the towering mountains and volcanoes further inland. Some of the creatures lurking on both land and sea were as vicious as any we had yet encountered and the ocean around us was many fathoms deep. Never had we felt so far from our homeland.

**1. Ropen** – This flying creature has bat wings; a long tail, split at the end like a fish; and a long beak filled with teeth. It eats decaying human flesh and lurks around human funerals. It is found on the Umboi and Manus islands near Papua New Guinea.

**2. Marawa** – Marawa is a great spider of Banks Island near Vanuatu. Marawa and his friend Qat, the creator spirit of Melanesia, both made humans. Qat made his people dance, but Marawa was so stunned when his people came to life that he buried them. They rotted and Marawa realised too late that he had invented death.

**3. Adaro** – These malevolent mer-people are found near the Solomon Islands. They have horns like the fins of a shark, spikes like a sword fish and tailfins for feet. Adaro shoot at humans with flying fish.

**4. Tui Delai Gau** – A peaceful giant of Gau Island, Fiji, Tui Delai Gau can take off his head and hands. The hands walk on their fingers, and hold up his head to see long distances.

**5. Tamangori** – This man-eating giant of the island of Mangaia in the Cook Islands, was defeated by two brothers. Because Tamangori moved silently, they could not find him. They roasted some rats, Tamangori's favourite food. He was drawn by the smell, ate the rats, then fell asleep. The brothers killed him while he slept.

**6. Te Tuna** – The eel demon, Te Tuna, was in love with Hina, a girl from the island of Tahiti in French Polynesia. When a massive flood came, he instructed her to cut off his head and bury it. From there grew the first coconut tree.

**7. Tumu-Ra'i-Fuena** – This gigantic octopus holds the Earth tight in his tentacles. He is also from Tahiti. When Rua, the god of war, tried to make the creature let go, his magic chants failed and the Earth remained safe.

**8. Mafuie** – The earthquake god, beaten in a wrestling match with the hero Ti'iti'i. The victor wrenched off Mafuie's arm but allowed him to keep the other in return for the secret of fire. Because Mafuie now has only one arm, Samoa's earthquakes are not as bad as they once were.

**9. Nanaue** – The son of a Hawaiian woman and the shark king, Nanaue, the shark man, was fed meat, which gave him a taste for human flesh.

**10. Kamapuaa** – Half-man, half-pig, Kamapuaa's snout snuffled out the mountains of Hawaii and his trotters dug vast lakes. When the goddess Pele rejected him, he travelled to the lowlands. Pele went to the hills, which she filled with volcanic fire.

**11. Mejenkwaad** – These female demons are found on the island of Airok in the Marshall Islands. They are created if a woman is left on her own after having a child.

*I know not where next our voyage will take us, for who knows what lies beyond the ends of the Earth.*

*The beasts haunt my nightmares and cloud my days. Not two hours ago, spying through my telescope a distant island, I saw a row of palm trees, crossed to form the dreaded signs:*

⟊⊙⊕⊤⟊⊻ ⟟⊻⟊⟊
⊕⟊⟟⊛⟊ ⟟⟊ ⊙⊤⟊⟊⊛
⊤⟊⊙ ⊤⊙⊙

*I am convinced I will never return to the lands of my youth.*

# 2 July, 1575, Great Walters Estate, Berkshire

Twelve years to the day after setting out from Southampton, I have finally reached home. Young Hal Hardacre has returned with me to the safety of the Walters Estate.

Safety? I had not settled but one hour before I noticed carvings above the great hall's fireplace that had not been there before. I examined them closely – and copy them here:

I searched back through my maps, and finally I understand. I know now what the beasts have been trying to tell me.

All has been for nothing. I have described the creatures that inhabit this planet to the best of my efforts and illustrated in great detail their wings, snouts, tails, fangs, talons, scales and hooves, yet all must be concealed – the monsters have spoken.

I cannot bring myself to destroy the fruits of such labour so I will seal them in a casket and entrust the box to Hal, who has become my most trusted friend. I grant him too my estates and my fortune. Henceforth the estate will be known as Hardacre Manor. I must live in hiding.

Hal's single instruction, and that of his descendants, is to conceal this most precious chest, even with their lives. If his family line should ever come to an end, I hope some hapless soul may not stumble upon the terrible secret.

For myself, I hope that I may live out my days in peace and put my quill to some good use. I enclose here my first poetic composition.

*Cornelius Walters*

### Lo the Kraken

Lo, how the Kraken howls through the storm,
Even like matchwood the ship meets its doom,
Yet I who have witnessed its terrible form
Must keep dumb and not speak of this monster of gloom.
Dire warnings they gave and I must take heed,
Delivered in cipher with infinite stealth:
"Keep silent of us and all of our breed
On pain of becoming a monster thyself."

By Cornelius Walters, 1575

Ruth Briggs
Librarian
Hardacre Manor
Berkshire

Mr. Edmund Wright, Editor
Mercator and Co
Mapmakers
Bloomsbury
London

9 December

Dear Mr Wright,

I write this in great haste. In your last letter you said that you would send Cornelius Walters' **Atlas of Monsters** to the printer this week. I now desperately hope you have not yet done so. I must exhort you not to continue with the project. The atlas must return to Hardacre Manor, to be resealed inside its trunk and perhaps even destroyed.

When I first read Walters's account of his travels, I assumed he had written a fantastical bestiary. Now, having spent many months studying his work in depth, I sincerely believe he was telling the truth.

We know from documents in the Hardacre family archive that the explorer did give a large fortune to one Henry Hardacre, a former cook's boy. Many have wondered why Walters turned his back on the world and passed his considerable wealth to a servant. Here, in a document no one was ever supposed to see, he explains everything.

Hal's family became wealthy and well-respected; my employer, the professor, was the last of the line, something Walters was concerned would one day lead to the chest being discovered, which indeed it was.

Yesterday evening I took one final look in the cavity where the chest had been concealed. Scratched into the wall were runes that were not there two days ago:

⚮⚲⊙ ⚺⊙⚳⚲⊕ ⚼⚺⚺ ⚳⊙⚿⊙⚴⚮⊙⚞
⚺⚺⚞⚻⚥ ⚻⚥⚺⚦ ⊛⚺⚮⚶⚶ Ψ⚲⚺⚞⊙
⚺⊙ ⚥⚺⚺

I have deciphered the message and now I know I must go away. I must run. I must hide. THEY ARE COMING.

*Ruth Briggs*

Edmund Wright, Editor
Mercator & Co
Mapmakers
Bloomsbury
London
United Kingdom

Ms R Briggs, Librarian
Hardacre Manor
Berkshire
United Kingdom

9 December

Dear Ms Briggs,

We have great pleasure in enclosing a copy of Cornelius Walters' *Atlas of Monsters*, which went on sale across the world today. There has been much interest and we are already considering a second print run.

One thing puzzles us. Yesterday a letter, which appears to be written in the strange script Walters records in his atlas, arrived in the post. Our experts are unable to make much of it; perhaps you can to shed some light on its meaning?

Yours Sincerely,

Edmund Wright, Editor

RECIPIENT UNKNOWN
AT THIS ADDRESS
RETURN TO SENDER

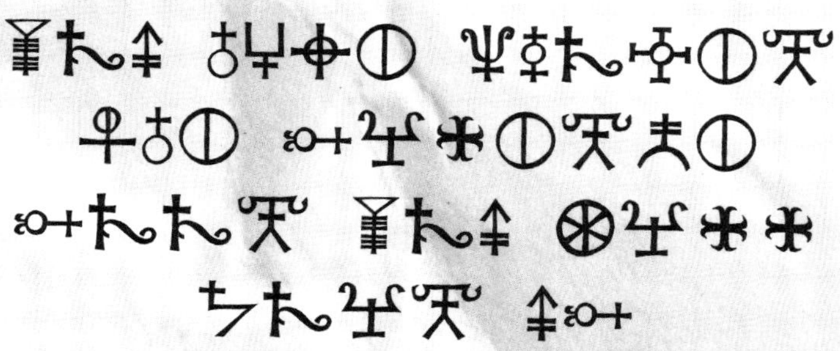

# Index of Monsters